An Unexpected Journal

The Imaginative Harvest of Holly Ordway

Advent 2021

Volume 4, Issue 4

Credits
Managing Editor: Zak Schmoll
Cover Art: Virginia De La Lastra
Journal Mark: Erika McMillan
Journal Design and Layout: Legacy Marketing Services
Editors: Carla Alvarez, Donald Catchings, Annie Crawford, Virginia de la Lastra, Karise Gililland, Ryan Grube, Sandra Hicks, Nicole Howe, Jason Monroe, Annie Nardone, Cherish Nelson, Megan Prahl, Zak Schmoll, Jason M. Smith, Rebekah Valerius
Contributors: Jesse W. Baker, Donald W. Catchings, Jr., Annie Crawford, Virginia de la Lastra, Ryan Grube, Seth Myers, Annie Nardone, Holly Ordway, Joseph Pearce, Josiah Peterson, Theresa Pihl, Jamie Danielle Portwood, Zak Schmoll, Jason M. Smith, Michael Ward, Clark Weidner, Donald T. Williams, Jared Zimmerer

Library of Congress ISSN
Digital: 2770-1174
Print: 2770-1166

An Unexpected Journal
Houston, TX

http://anunexpectedjournal.com
Email: anunexpectedjournal@gmail.com

CONTENTS

An Interview with Holly Ordway

On *Tolkien's Modern Reading* and Cultural Apologetics

In order to detail Tolkien's modern literary influences, you had to read as many of the books Tolkien had read as you could — which means first you had to play detective and discover what works he read. What provoked you to take up this massive challenge?

The short answer is: intellectual curiosity!

I've been interested in Tolkien and his work ever since I read *The Hobbit* and *The Lord of the Rings* as a young girl, and read "On Fairy-stories" as a teenager; the latter experience, I realize now, is what inspired me to become an academic and a literary critic myself. I've been thinking seriously about his work for more than thirty years. Ten years ago, I realized that there were some very interesting questions about *The Lord of the Rings* to which I couldn't find satisfactory answers. So I decided to investigate.

The first question was "How much did Tolkien read of the modern fantasy authors who came before *The Lord of the Rings*? And what did he think of their work?"

I wrote my doctoral dissertation on the development of the modern fantasy novel, which entailed reading massive amounts of fantasy literature from the Victorians up to Tolkien, and then from Tolkien through the 1990s. Tolkien had such a strong influence on the writers who came after him that it's now almost impossible to conceive of the genre without him — and this can obscure just how innovative and distinctive *The Lord of the Rings* was. It was fascinating to discover the diversity of pre-Tolkienian modern fantasy (writers like Lord Dunsany, E.R. Eddison, William Morris, H.P. Lovecraft, and Robert Howard) and by this comparison to see Tolkien's work from a fresh perspective.

From Tolkien's essay "On Fairy-stories" and the *Letters*, I knew of his familiarity with at least some modern authors of fantasy; I began to wonder how many he had read, and whether they had influenced him. There was enough scholarship out there to suggest that this was an area worth exploring, yet nothing that fully answered my question.

The second question was "How can we account for the power of *The Lord of the Rings* for modern readers if we assume that it's basically medieval in inspiration?"

I had accepted that Tolkien was fundamentally and exclusively a medievalist, at best indifferent to the modern world and modern culture. After all, his own authorized biographer, Humphrey Carpenter, definitively stated in his group biography of the Inklings that "the major names in twentieth-century writing meant little or nothing to [Tolkien]. He read very little modern fiction, and took no serious notice of it." I was untroubled by this image of my favorite author: in fact, it was largely responsible for my initial desire to be a medievalist myself. (I started my graduate studies in Old and Middle English, with a particular interest in the Arthurian legends.)

But if Tolkien had been such a thoroughgoing medievalist, how did he manage to make *The Lord of the Ring* speak so powerfully to the issues and concerns of the 20th and then the 21st century? Furthermore, I realized that Tolkien's writing style has distinctively *modern* characteristics; this was especially clear in comparison to William Morris, whose fantasies are essentially pastiches of medieval literature, archaic language and all. Tolkien was clearly using medieval materials, but something else was going on as well. I began to wonder about Tolkien's engagement with modern culture in general. Was he perhaps more widely read than I had hitherto assumed?

These questions had been in the back of my mind for years. Then, in a relatively short span of time, I read two important books that opened up new possibilities. Diana Pavlac Glyer's *The Company They Keep: C.S. Lewis and J.R.R. Tolkien as Writers in Community* showed that the prevailing view of Tolkien as immune to influence was incorrect. If that assumption was over-simplistic, perhaps so too was the idea that he was only interested in medieval language and literature. John Garth's *Tolkien and the Great War* showed that Tolkien had been profoundly influenced by that most modern of catastrophes, World War I.

And so, finally, I thought to myself, "These are interesting questions. I think I'll try to find some answers." Little did I know what I was getting myself into!

This undertaking took you a decade. How would you compare your conception of the project at its inception to its completed form?

My initial idea for the book was titled *Tolkien Before and After*: since I didn't expect to have much material with regard to his modern reading, I intended the second half of the book to address his subsequent influence on other writers. Obviously, that's not the book that I ended up writing! One of the essentials of good research is that you have to follow the material where it takes you, even if it means radically overhauling your original plans.

I revised my approach and adopted the working title of *Tolkien's Modern Sources*. Then I realized that there was so much material that, to keep it manageable, I had to focus exclusively on the "certains" — the books for which I had evidence that Tolkien knew or at least owned them. The distinction between "certain" and "probable" is a vital one in this book. Scholars can indeed productively talk about the "probables," but it's important to be precise and clear about what things we have evidence for and what things are the subject of speculation or hypothesis.

Even then, the book took another turn. I had to reckon with the fact that Carpenter was simply incorrect about Tolkien's attitude toward modern literature, and he was mistaken in other ways that arguably affected the accuracy of his portrait of Tolkien. Normally, one biographer's over-generalizations about his subject would not be a big deal, but in this case, it is. Tolkien has been the subject of few major biographies compared to other contemporary literary figures of equal significance, and most of Tolkien's biographers base their work on Carpenter's biography. Consider, for instance, that Robert Frost, Tolkien's almost exact contemporary, has had at least four major biographies that, to various degrees, challenge or correct each other's interpretations of Frost's personality and writings; the same is the case for C.S. Lewis. I researched what Carpenter himself had said about his work on Tolkien and the Inklings, and I looked at the history of scholarship on Tolkien as a modern writer, finding that before Carpenter's biographies, scholars were much more likely to consider Tolkien alongside other modern authors.

To be sure, a good many Tolkien scholars had already noted various errors and biases in Carpenter's work, and many had written thoughtfully about exceptions to the apparent rule of Tolkien's lack of interest in modern literature; however, the various pieces hadn't been fitted together into a whole picture. Certainly, the wider public view of Tolkien was as a Luddite, a man stuck in the past. I felt that my argument would be incomplete if I didn't at least try to address how and why this faulty perception arose and has persisted. This line of investigation eventually led me to realize that multiple factors were involved — including Tolkien's own self-presentation! It's an enormously complex topic and I'm sure that I haven't gotten to the bottom of it, but I hope that my work will stimulate more research and analysis from a fresh perspective.

Eventually I realized the book had to be called *Tolkien's Modern Reading*, because "Sources" was too limiting. For one thing, I had come to realize that Tolkien engaged creatively with his reading in many different ways: sometimes as source-material, yes, but we can also trace more subtle modes of influence, including what I call influence-by-opposition, in which his dislike or disapproval of something he read prompted him to show how it ought to be done! (*Smith of Wootton Major* is the prime example of the latter, as Tolkien himself explains that it is a reaction against George MacDonald's "The Golden Key.") I also realized that even when there isn't a direct influence to be traced, Tolkien's interest in modern literature — what he read, what he thought about it — sheds a great deal of light on his personality and his creative process.

In 2011, I had not the slightest idea that I'd end up drawing these conclusions. It's been an exciting journey of discovery, and I am profoundly grateful for the opportunity to have taken it.

Given your now considerable understanding of Tolkien's reading habits, his literary inputs, and his approach to (sub)creating stories, have you been able to glean any new or surprising insights about Tolkien in light of your research?

Many! Let me name just three.

I discovered that Tolkien read and admired the work of many female authors, including Mary Renault, Agatha Christie, Beatrix Potter, and Edith Nesbit -- and that he had a wider range of female friendships and academic collaborators than is usually assumed. As just one example, he was good friends with Dorothy Everett and Elaine Griffiths, two of his Oxford faculty colleagues. Much ink has been spilled on the subject of the Inklings being a male-only group, but hitherto no one seems to have realized that "The Cave," an Oxford literary and social club that Tolkien co-founded, had both female and male members (including Everett, Griffiths, and other women academics).

I also learned that it's simply not true that Tolkien hated Narnia! To be sure, he wasn't enthusiastic about *The Lion, the Witch and the Wardrobe* (we must allow for personal taste) but the idea that he hated the books or was jealous of Lewis for their ease of composition is incorrect. In fact, he later called the Narnia Chronicles “deservedly very popular.”

Lastly, one of my most intriguing discoveries was a gradual realization of the significance of the sheer *Englishness* of Tolkien’s personality. I spend about three months of the year in Oxford, and have done so for more than a decade now, and over the years I’ve gradually come to a greater and greater awareness of the subtle ways in which the English differ from Americans in their mode of expression. For instance, Tolkien is characteristically English in the way that he tends to be hyperbolic about the things that he dislikes or disagrees with, but self-deprecating and understated in talking about what he most values or finds important (for the English, ‘not bad’ is a term of high praise).

In Not God’s Type, you mention an aversion to the kind of literary criticism that treats stories and poems “as language games,” going so far as to say it was one of the reasons you wrote your doctoral dissertation “on the little-regarded genre of fantasy.” Does the academic study of literature always tend to squelch its appeal? Are certain genres — such as fantasy — more immune than others from such a tendency?

Sadly, the academic study of literature does have the potential to squelch or even destroy one's appreciation of the subject. There's a certain type of literary critic who tends to view enjoyment of literature as a kind of childishness, a sign of shallowness and lack of critical insight, and many academic works of literary criticism are written in a kind of insider jargon that is neither intelligible nor interesting to anyone outside that particular small corner of the academy. Too often, literary studies also means making literature fit the Procrustean bed of whatever theoretical or socio-political views are fashionable at the moment. None of this fosters love and appreciation for literature as something (dare we say it!) that we *enjoy*.

Fortunately, it doesn't have to be this way — and indeed this attitude is, historically speaking, an aberration. Samuel Johnson, possibly the greatest critic in the history of English literature, certainly didn't take this sort of sterile approach! C.S. Lewis was an outstanding literary critic, among his other gifts (*An Experiment in Criticism* is a must-read). Tolkien himself models, in "On Fairy-stories," an approach to literature that is fundamentally appreciative even while it is intellectually rigorous.

When I began my doctoral studies, I thought that the only way to avoid doing the sort of literary criticism that "murders by dissection" was to focus on a genre that had escaped much attention from literary theorists. That's no longer the case for fantasy, but I also no longer feel that hiding away is the right reaction. Turning inward can be tempting, as a protective measure, but it can also lead to a reluctance to think critically and deeply about one's favorite texts and authors. In the end, bad scholarship will fade away, but good scholarship will endure — if we do the scholarship. If we leave literary criticism to be done by those who *don't* love what they read, then of course we won't be happy with the results!

This leads me to note that one of the most important influences on *Tolkien's Modern Reading* is Michael Ward's *Planet Narnia*. Not only does Michael present a compelling and well-argued thesis that is, in my view, completely convincing, he also writes in beautifully clear and elegant prose that is a pleasure to read. What's more, this book both illuminates its subject and enhances appreciation of it: after I read *Planet Narnia*, I re-read the Narnia Chronicles and found that not only did I understand them more deeply, I enjoyed them even more fully than I had before. That, in my mind, is the gold standard of literary criticism. Michael showed me that it can be done, and that it is worth doing.

Tolkien's influence on fantasy has been so comprehensive that the genre is now almost over-saturated with Lord of the Rings derivatives (from Dungeons & Dragons to made-up languages to memes). But then, The Hobbit has been characterized as Beowulf fan-fiction. What is the difference between pop-culture mashups and Tolkien's creative integration of material from various sources?

I think the key difference is expressed in the word "integration." Tolkien himself used the image of "leaf-mould" for the material that nourished his creative imagination. The brown, fertile mulch that we find on the forest floor is made up of leaves fallen from many trees that, over time, break down and enrich the soil, with nutrients eventually drawn up into the tree to form new leaves. Tolkien's own "Tree of Tales" was nourished by leaves from trees across centuries, indeed millennia, and it grew over time. There was nothing hasty about Tolkien's imaginative growth!

Pop-culture mashups derive much of their interest from the reader recognizing their components and enjoying the clever or funny juxtapositions that the creator has made. Therefore, they're always going to be evanescent. What is staler than last year's favorite meme — or last week's?

(Interestingly, Tolkien did write something that could be called "*Beowulf* fan-fiction," and it's the story "Sellic Spell": his attempt to imagine the folktale that was source-material for the *Beowulf*-poet. It appears in his *Beowulf: A Translation and Commentary*.)

The authors of imitative works have often been profoundly and genuinely moved by *The Lord of the Rings*, but what they are aiming at is, in effect, to re-create the experience of a favorite book. Once the appeal of "this gives me an experience *similar to* my favorite book" wears off, the derivative work doesn't have enough of its own merit to last.

Creative integration is essential for a work that stands on its own and holds up over time. And as we consider Tolkien's own creative imagination, we should remember that it wasn't just his reading that contributed to nourishing his Tree of Tales, but also his life experiences, his faith, his scholarly work, his friendships, his very environment. Part of Tolkien's genius is in the way that he assimilates and integrates all these elements, making something that is uniquely his own.

In 2017 you published Apologetics and the Christian Imagination which essentially explained and unpacked Lewis's claim that "reason is the natural organ of truth; but the imagination is the organ of meaning. Imagination . . . is not the cause of truth but its condition." Your book showed how metaphors create the meaning necessary for evaluating truth and applied this principle to several important apologetic topics such as the incarnation and the problem of pain. Where do you see the culture in 2021 most misunderstanding the meaning of Christianity?

I think that one of the basic and most significant issues has to do with the meaning of *choice*. I would say that one of the basic misunderstandings is that Christianity is seen as a belief system that one can choose or reject, in whole or in part, rather than as an account of reality that may be true or false. And I think this is important to note because Christians are also part of the culture; this is not a problem for "those people out there" but also for "us in here."

Choice — the ability to say 'this, and not that' to anything and everything — has become increasingly a dominant and harmful feature of our culture. To be sure, the ability to make meaningful choices is indeed a basic part of what it means to be human; we are moral beings precisely because we can, within certain limits, choose between right and wrong, good and evil, in any given situation. But our ability to choose is neither arbitrary nor infinite. We can choose between right and wrong because there *are* such things as right and wrong, and they are not of our making. Objective value is real, and is accessible to every human being at some level, even without divine revelation to clarify, guide, and deepen our understanding of the moral law. (That's why C.S. Lewis's prescient book *The Abolition of Man* is increasingly important for us today!) There are other things that are 'given' and not chosen, including the basic fact of being born at all. A person can (tragically) choose to end his or her life, but cannot choose never to have existed at all. Ultimately, we must all come to grips with the existentially terrifying fact that, as Bishop Robert Barron puts it, "your life is not about you."

I venture to suspect that at least some of what is identified as "relativism" among the religiously non-affiliated or the "spiritual but not religious" is an over-application of this emphasis on choice. After all, if we tell young people repeatedly, "you can be *anything* you want to be!", it's not unreasonable that they'll internalize this not simply as (rather bad) career advice, but as a basic truth about the way the world works. People do learn what we teach them; it's just that sometimes we don't realize exactly what we're teaching.

That's why I have increasingly been emphasizing, when I speak or write about the importance of meaning-making in apologetics and evangelization, the need for every Christian to strive for a life of personal holiness. Insofar as we, individually, are able to internalize what it means to be a Christian — to conform to *reality*, not just our personal preferences — to that degree our witness will be more effective. The Christian faith is true, however flawed its messengers are, but one of the most convincing indications that it *is* true is the extent to which our lives are in accord with the reality we proclaim.

As St Philip Neri said, "The great thing is to become saints"! Fortunately, he also advised that "we must not wish to do everything at once, or become a saint in four days." We must be patient with ourselves, and persevere as we try to grow in holiness, to love God with all our heart, soul, mind, and strength, and our neighbors as ourselves.

A decade ago, you were already in the vanguard of what is now broadly known as cultural or imaginative apologetics, and you have spent the better part of that time working with leaders in the field and training future apologists. How has the specifically cultural/imaginative aspect impacted the public square? Where do you perceive God is making good use of cultural/imaginative apologists?

I have been greatly encouraged by the steady increase in attention to cultural, imaginative, and literary modes of apologetics in the last few years. From the academic to the widely popular level, we're seeing more books that take the imagination seriously, or at least give it an acknowledgement! I've also noticed more Christians reviewing secular films, music, and books in ways that thoughtfully engage with the culture: discerning what does and does not accord with the faith, yes, but not in a dismissive or harshly judgmental way: rather, in a way that looks for ways to plant and water the "seeds of the Word" in the wider culture. This is an extremely positive development. If we are to share the good news of the Gospel, we need to meet people where they are. Where else can we possibly meet them?

The impact of cultural and imaginative apologetics is deepened, I believe, by the fact that it's taking root ecumenically. I think we can see God's grace at work in the way that this approach to apologetics and evangelization is growing stronger in both Evangelical Protestant and Catholic contexts. For instance, HBU's work in apologetics is continuing to thrive and grow, and I'm honored to continue to have a connection as Visiting Professor. And it's fitting that, in my work now for the Word on Fire Institute, my title is the Cardinal Francis George Fellow of Faith and Culture. Faith *and* culture!

I venture to say that imaginative approaches are resonating with people precisely because we live in a culture that is starved of real meaning. People are grasping at anything that seems to offer some significance to their lives — and all too often, settling on alluring but ultimately insubstantial, unsatisfying, or even poisonous substitutes. Helping people discover meaning in *reality*, with all its natural and supernatural splendor, is a massive, even daunting endeavor, but it's the work at hand. We may be tempted to say, like Frodo, "I wish this need not have happened in our time," but we must heed Gandalf's reply: "So do I, and so do all who live to see such times. But that is not for them to decide. All we have to decide is what to do with the time that is given us."

Finally, I would say that one of the most beautiful aspects of the rise of cultural and imaginative apologetics is that, in my observation, it is growing in the context of community. Etymologically, the word "culture" derives from the

Latin *cultura*, meaning the tending of crops. It is related to the word "cult" in the sense of "system of religious worship." which derives ultimately from the Latin *cultus*, which includes among its meanings the tilling of the earth. Faith and culture are thus linguistically rooted in an activity, agriculture, that requires a community working together for planting, tending, and harvest — sharing hard work and seasonal feasting.

The work of *An Unexpected Journal* is itself a beautiful example of this kind of work in community. It is one of the greatest gifts to a teacher to see students going out into the world, using and building upon what they have learned. And my students have given a great deal back to me, as well, in helping me to shape and refine my work. For instance, my next book, *Tales of Faith* (planned to release in summer 2022) is a discussion guide for using ancient and medieval literature for evangelization and discipleship. It is an answer to the question that my HBU students often asked me: "When will you write a book based on your teaching?" It is a book designed *for* community, that arises *from* community.

Indeed, in my own work as a writer and academic, I am extraordinarily blessed to have people in my life who provide encouragement, feedback, practical help, fellowship, and friendship. This kind of community is vital both for doing the work that we have at hand and for our emotional, intellectual, and spiritual health. We can't, and shouldn't, and mustn't, try to go it alone. Let's help each other to become saints

REVIEW: *TOLKIEN'S MODERN READING*

Annie Crawford on a Challenge to Tolkien Scholarship

Long before the printing press, Solomon complained that "of the making of many books there is no end, and much study is a weariness of the flesh."[1] What would Solomon say in the day of blogs and self-publishing? Yet despite the flood of Too Much Information, we at *An Unexpected Journal* still believe there are things worth saying, new wisdom yet to be written, and greater understanding worth seeking out on the printed page, and we are pleased to recommend Holly Ordway's new ground-breaking *Tolkien's Modern Reading* as just such a book. We are glad Cicero kept writing in his age of Too Many Books, and we are glad that scholars like Ordway work hard to cut through the noise of half-baked scholarship to offer something truly great. The fruit of ten years' careful research, *Tolkien's*

[1] Ecclesiastes 12:12

Modern Reading is worthy of serving as the flagship book for Word on Fire's new academic imprint.

Ordway's new academic masterpiece holds special significance for us at AUJ. The founders and editors at *An Unexpected Journal* are alumni from the Houston Baptist University Cultural Apologetics Program, which Holly Ordway largely built and developed during her time as Program Coordinator and Chair of the Department of Apologetics. While in the HBU program, all of us at AUJ were profoundly impacted by Professor Ordway's high standards of excellence, first-rate scholarship, gifted teaching, and active mentorship. It is no overstatement to say that Ordway's investment in her HBU students is a primary reason that *An Unexpected Journal* exists. For us, reading *Tolkien's Modern Reading* is very much like being in one of our favorite classes again. In this book, an expert scholar and teacher, with genuine love for her subject and reader, leads you through a literary world of characters, motifs, and themes, modeling how to think critically, showing you how to be diligent and thorough in your research, and helping you see how small details can have great significance. Ordway writes as she teaches — with a fierce Eowyn-like power and love. Ordway challenges her students because she loves them, and in her new book, Ordway challenges Tolkien scholarship because she loves it.

Beyond its general excellence, *Tolkien's Modern Reading* marks an important turning point in Tolkien scholarship. To date, scholars and lay enthusiasts alike focused their analysis primarily on the obvious medieval influences for Middle-earth. Tolkien was a professor of Anglo-Saxon literature, and it doesn't take much expertise to see the influence that *Beowulf* and other medieval legends and romances had on *The Hobbit* and *The Lord of The Rings*. Indeed, it is so widely assumed that Middle-earth is *merely* rooted in the medieval world that some secondary schools place Tolkien's work in their medieval Great Text classes. Though written in the twentieth century, *The Lord of the Rings* is thus being studied *as* a medieval text.

Ordway started her research into Tolkien's influences by taking this general consensus as her own, yet the evidence itself led her to other conclusions. As she investigated the boundaries of Tolkien's reading habits, Ordway discovered to her surprise that they were very broad and significantly modern. The more she hunted down Tolkien's personal reading list and scoured his private bookshelves, the more she realized that Tolkien, even more than his friend C.S. Lewis, was engaged with modern literary works and inspired by them.

In retrospect, this should not surprise us. *The Lord of the Rings* indeed deserves to be in the Great Text curriculum, but not as a medieval book, for the Great Books of western culture are great precisely because they both draw on the masterpieces that preceded them and speak universal truths with fresh wisdom to their own contemporary world. When Dante wrote *The Divine Comedy*, it was a very "contemporary" book, in the sense that it spoke with cutting-edge creativity and relevance to the culture in which it was birthed.

Likewise, *The Lord of the Rings* both draws from the great stories of the English past, such as *Beowulf*, and speaks universal truths with new creative form and insight that is distinctly modern. The most obvious example of Tolkien's modernity is the literary form of *The Hobbit* and *The Lord of the Rings*: novels are distinctly modern. Medieval storytellers didn't work in long pages of descriptive prose, they didn't create such complex plots, nor did they spend much time on the psychological and relational development of their characters; these are the interests of the leisured modern man. Moreover, many of Tolkien's themes have distinctly modern characters as well. Although medieval stories almost always connected the virtue of the king to the health of his land, ancient and medieval men did not have the technological anxieties that Tolkien weaves into his portrayal of Isengard. No Anglo-Saxon author could have imagined or written *The Lord of the Rings*, illustrating how much both the modern and the medieval shaped the furniture of Tolkien's imagination.

Ordway opens *Tolkien's Modern Reading* with a precisely crafted thesis: "Tolkien knew modern literature, and was oriented toward the modern world, to a greater degree than we have hitherto realized. Acknowledging this aspect of his creative process will enhance our ability to interpret and enjoy his work."[2] Ordway makes the limits of her claim clear: "I shall not be arguing that his modern reading is *more* important than his medieval reading . . . [it] is undoubtedly a relatively minor element in the total picture. But it is present and should not be overlooked."[3] Ordway does not overstate her own position in order to counterweight portrayals of Tolkien as merely a stodgy medievalist; rather, she carefully leads us into a more fruitful, multi-

---

[2] Holly Ordway, *Tolkien's Modern Reading: Middle-earth Beyond the Middle Ages* (Park Ridge, IL: Word on Fire Academic, 2021), 9.

[3] Ibid.

dimensional picture of Tolkien's personality and literary influences.

The first chapter of *Tolkien's Modern Reading* describes the backdrop of contemporary Tolkien scholarship which, under Humphrey Carpenter's influence, tends to reduce Tolkien to a fossilized medievalist. Ordway's research revealed claims made by Carpenter which were simply factually incorrect. Searching through various articles and interviews, Ordway learned that Carpenter didn't especially like Tolkien and felt free as a biographer to sketch the man in a reductive way that suited his own anti-religious, anti-medieval biases. In an article suspiciously titled "Learning about Ourselves: Biography as Autobiography," Carpenter admits to writing a "caricature of the Oxford academic" and that his biographical approach was focused on smashing idols.[4] He believed that "around each figure there's an absurd cult of admirers, people who want the great person to remain untarnished. And it's a challenge to try and tarnish them."[5] This was evidently the approach Carpenter took when writing Tolkien's biography,

---

[4] Humphrey Carpenter, "Learning about Ourselves: Biography as Autobiography," in *The Art of Literary Biography*, ed. John Bachelor (Oxford: Clarendon, 1995), 270.

[5] Carpenter, "Learning about Ourselves," 273, 275.

for Christopher Tolkien rejected Carpenter's first draft as offensively slapstick.[6] However, Carpenter only took two weeks to revise the book, indicating that he simply removed some of the more directly offensive descriptions but did not fundamentally re-write his portrait of Tolkien to be more sympathetic.[7] Ordway outlines the primary misconceptions that Carpenter's tarnished portrait created and shows why now "the picture of Tolkien as fundamentally backward-looking, happily living in total rejection of the modern world, must be abandoned."[8]

In chapter two, Ordway meticulously lays out the precise scope of her thesis, explains her research methods, and details the focus and boundaries of the evidence she has collected. Ordway limits the sources she considers to the fiction, poetry, and drama written after 1850 that we are certain Tolkien read. She also limits herself to sources that had influence on the Middle-earth legendarium. Acknowledging that "source-hunting" can be a specious business which implies "that identifying the sources of a tale revealed everything worth

---

[6] Ordway, *Tolkien's Modern Reading*, 10.

[7] Ibid., 11.

[8] Ibid., 24.

knowing about it,"[9] Ordway explains how her research into Tolkien's sources is "not seeking to crack riddles but to plumb the depths of imagination."[10] Following the best principles of literary analysis, Ordway does not reduce elements of Tolkien's work to specific influences, but rather shows how an understanding of his influences can expand and enrich our understanding of Tolkien's imagination, stories, and significance.

Ordway supports her thesis in subsequent chapters with a truly mountainous collection of evidence organized by either genre or author. Even with the limitations Ordway placed on her project to keep it manageable, the scope of her research and of Tolkien's own reading is astounding, encompassing a total of over 200 titles and 148 different authors, including authors as diverse as Matthew Arnold, W.H. Auden, Hilaire Belloc, Wendall Berry, Mark Twain, Lewis Carroll, L. Frank Baum, Oscar Wilde, Agatha Christie, G.K. Chesterton, H. Rider Haggard, T.S. Eliot, E.R. Eddison, Kenneth Grahame, Andrew Lang, George MacDonald, Rudyard Kipling, P.G. Wodehouse, Arthur Ransome, Beatrix Potter, William Morris, A.A. Milne, and scores more.

[9] Ordway, *Tolkien's Modern Reading*, 40.

[10] Ibid., 39.

Although the 2019 *Tolkien's Library* covers much of the same ground as Ordway's book, it is not much more than an annotated bibliography. *Tolkien's Modern Reading* is a landmark volume in Tolkien scholarship because of the meaningful and persuasive analysis Ordway draws from Tolkien's modern reading list. For over a decade, Ordway dug into every available detail of Tolkien's life, collecting tiny pieces of literary evidence which she painstakingly pieced together into a complex mosaic of Tolkien's immense and fecund imagination.

Tolkien's Modern Reading concludes with a summary of Ordway's argument, a final deconstruction of Humphrey Carpenter's most influential yet misleading claims, and a call for Tolkien scholars to leave behind the idea that Tolkien was an impervious medieval bandersnatch stuck in the irrelevant past and instead enter a new era of exploration into the life and work of this multifaceted, genius, and immeasurably important modern author.

Nearly a fourth of the book provides scholarly resources for further study. In the appendix, Ordway includes a chart that details a comprehensive list of everything we know Tolkien read, organized by where Ordway found the information — whether from writings, letters, interviews, images of his bookshelf, books on a syllabus he taught, or first-hand reports from others. An extended photo gallery enriches this study with a visualization of the modern sources Tolkien read. The illustrations of scenes and characters like the Snergs, MacDonald's goblins, Fafnir the Dragon, the knight in *John Inglesant* allow us to see and not just read about the influences these modern creations had on the stories of Middle-earth. *Tolkien's Modern Reading* also includes a well-developed index and comprehensive bibliography, making this volume an essential and highly usable resource for fans and scholars alike. Throughout the book, Ordway provides extensive footnotes that include interesting anecdotes, connections, asides, nuances, and important sources for extended research. Each chapter ends with a wonderfully helpful summary of the primary points; for the lay reader, these ending summaries provide help from Professor Ordway who wants to make sure you caught the key points, and for the scholar who never has enough time to read everything they ought, the summaries offer a excellent time-saving resource. From cover to cover, *Tolkien's Modern Reading* embodies the rigorous academic standards we at AUJ would expect from a professor who constantly told us to verify our information, pay attention to the quality of bibliographies, and follow the citation trail.

Although highly academic, Ordway's gifts as a storyteller and teacher make the entire book highly readable. Her prose is pristine and the well-paced dance between specific, lively details and generalized themes and conclusions keeps this work of research well-paced and engaging. Frankly, at times the unfolding drama of a great man misunderstood — complete with rogue biographies, professional intrigues, and scholarly confessions — reads almost like a novel. Ordway's research always stays rooted in the life of a real man with a meaningful story to tell.

As Ordway develops her argument, her teaching gifts shine through her analysis of the various texts, providing the reader with a bonus course in literary theory along with the Tolkien literary tour. From adventure stories to fables, from poetry to science fiction, from children's fantasy to sophisticated works like James Joyce's *Finnegans Wake*, Ordway guides her reader through important modern genres and authors. As she explains how different authors influenced the style, themes, setting, tone, and language of Tolkien's fiction, Ordway is teaching you how to read, what elements to look for in a story, how creative processes work, how stories communicate meaning, and how to evaluate the quality of a story.

A few times Ordway's source hunting feels stretched, as though the habit of making connections leads her to see ghosts of influence that aren't clearly there. Some faulty speculation is inevitable, for as Tolkien himself explains, his stories grow "like a seed in the dark out of the leaf-mould of the mind: out of all that has been seen or thought or read, that has long ago been forgotten, descending into the deeps."[11] There in the depths of the imagination, elements from Tolkien's own reading are "incorporated not in a conscious or deliberate way, but as fully digested and assimilated material in Tolkien's own imagination."[12] Literal compost is so completely broken down that it is impossible to reconstruct its constituents so as to isolate and identify the specific plants from which one handful might come. Likewise, if the elements of Tolkien's reading are so deeply digested in the unconscious imagination, then the ability to draw direct and specific connections will be at times impossible and unhelpful.

---

[11] Quoted in Ordway, *Tolkien's Modern Reading*, 8.

[12] Ibid., 86.

For example, when discussing *The Wind in the Willows,* Ordway speculates that Tolkien was "recalling Toad's tasty stew, eaten on the run in a gipsy's campsite, when Sam cooks his herbs and stewed rabbit."[13] This seems a stretch as the image of cooking during outdoor journeys is a common human experience and present in many stories. Tolkien need not read Graham Greene to imagine what it was like to cook dinner on a trek through remote and hostile country. All our stories bear common elements not simply because they have all directly influenced one another but primarily because they all bear witness to a common world. However, such strained influences are rare in the book and even if a fair number of Ordway's tentative connections were not actually present in the workings of Tolkien's imagination, she still has an ample amount of clear evidence to support her limited thesis.

As the title suggests, *Tolkien's Modern Reading* also offers the reader not only an overview of Tolkien's influences but also an overview of modern literature, much of which is commonly neglected in literary circles and literature classes today. If you are a teacher, homeschool educator, or avid reader

[13] Ordway, *Tolkien's Modern Reading*, 86.

looking to update your syllabus or expand your bookshelf, Ordway's book will serve as a helpful guide. As we learn about the similarities between Éowyn and William Morris's heroine Hall-Sun, the inspiration for Hobbits found in Wyke-Smith's Snergs, Nesbit's influence on Tolkien's plotting, and the precursors of Mordor found in MacDonald's "The Golden Key," our love for Tolkien's Middle-earth becomes a portal into many more worthwhile stories. As we learn the modern sources for names and places like "Crack of Doom" and the "Dead Marshes" and the "root of the mountains," Ordway shows us how many of the themes in *The Lord of the Rings* come not from medieval stories but modern ones. For example, the way Tolkien develops what Ordway describes as "perhaps the key theme" of *The Lord of the Rings* — the power of compassion to serve as the climactic catalyst — appears to be inspired by J.H. Shorthouse's modern novel, *John Inglesant.*[14] A discerning and trustworthy guide, Ordway read every source herself, and she helps the reader discern the wheat from the chaff, leading us to new treasures worth recovering from the early twentieth century dustbin — like the works of Wyke-Smiths, John Buchan, and Rider Haggard — and letting us

[14] Ordway, *Tolkien's Modern Reading,* 247.

know which volumes are better left in it — like the racist works of Alexander MacDonald.

Through our tour of *Tolkien's Modern Reading,* we may be surprised to discover that there are many enjoyable stories to be found in the modern era. Much of what we read in our modern literature courses is filtered through a particular bias in favor of books with philosophical significance. Modern Literature syllabi usually cover authors like Joyce, Kafka, Woolf, Eliot, Faulkner, Hemingway, and Beckett to reveal the increasing nihilism of the post-war era. These authors are important, but limiting the syllabus in this way does little to inspire most students to read more modern literature, and it misrepresents the wealth of literary variety that existed from 1880-1960. Thus, *Tolkien's Modern Reading* not only sheds light on Middle-earth, it may be that Middle-earth sheds a redemptive light back onto the world of modern literature. Tolkien's own reading may offer an important guide for re-writing our syllabi to include more adventure, mystery, fantasy, and science fiction which can help students become better, happier readers as well as see that, in the words of Ordway's favorite poet, Gerard Manley Hopkins, "though the last lights off the black west went" still "morning, at the brown brink eastward, springs."[15]

Holly Ordway's *Tolkien's Modern Reading* deserves a place on your overflowing bookshelf. It is an important corrective to the deconstructivist trends in Tolkien scholarship that began with Humphrey Carpenter's self-centered attempt to caricature his Christian subject as a "tweedy, nostalgic medievalist who read little or nothing of modern literature."[16] The impulse to portray Tolkien as retrograde and locked in the dark ages of Christendom functionally diminishes his ability to speak to our modern world. If we can limit Tolkien's imagination to an age that we may feel nostalgia for but have rejected as holding serious wisdom, then we can likewise treat the Christian themes of *The Lord of the Rings* as entertaining but ultimately irrelevant. We can enjoy Tolkien as escapist fantasy without worrying that he speaks with authority to our contemporary reality. The more I can see dragons as imaginary relics from an archaic, misguided past, the less I have to worry that Smaug

[15] Cited from Holly Ordway and Daniel Seseske, eds., *Ignatian Collection* (Park RIdge, IL: Word on Fire, 2020), 179.

[16] Ordway, *Tolkien's Modern Reading*, 249.

has something to say about the greed of my own heart.

In *Tolkien's Modern Reading*, Ordway proves that Tolkien was very much a man of the 20th century who could draw from the wisdom of the past to speak prophetically to our present. The proof is in the pudding: Tolkien made medieval motifs wildly popular to twentieth century people. He interpreted the medieval world for his modern readers in a way that resonated deeply, and "an interpreter must know both cultures, the old and the new."[17]

Perhaps more than ever, the old holds the necessary keys to a new future. We need Tolkien. His voice is not fossilized or antiquated; his fiction draws from the wisdom of the past to embody for present age the living Logos that was and is and ever shall be.

[17] Ordway, *Tolkien's Modern Reading*, 20.

Peak Middle-earth: Why Mount Doom is not the Climax of The *Lord of the Rings*

Michael Ward on Tolkien's Unobvious High Point

Peter Jackson's film version of Tolkien's *The Return of the King* was a huge commercial and critical success, winning all eleven Academy Awards for which it was nominated. However, it was not immune from criticism even as it received its bouquets. "Eleven nominations!" declared Billy Crystal in his opening monologue at the 2004 Oscars. "Yes, *eleven* nominations, — one for each ending!"

The end of the movie appears as if it might have been reached when the screen goes black after the destruction of the Ring and the eruption of Mount Doom. But, of course, there is more to come as Frodo and Sam are rescued by the eagles. The screen then turns white. Perhaps this is the end? No, Frodo awakes to discover that Gandalf is alive; he is then reunited with the other surviving members of the Fellowship. Is *this* the end? No, for the scene now shifts to Minas Tirith where Aragorn is crowned king. The coronation throng bows to the four hobbits and a map appears on screen signaling their return to the Shire. They go for a drink in the pub. Sam marries Rosie Cotton. Frodo writes an account of his adventures.

And still the movie is not over. "There's room for a little more," as Frodo says, handing Sam the book for him to add his own chapters later. At which point we embark on yet another journey, this time to the Grey Havens, where Gandalf oversees Frodo's painful parting from his three hobbit friends.

And even then there's one last thing to show: the return of Sam to the bosom of his family in Hobbiton. "Well, I'm back," he says. Finally, finally, finally, the film finishes.

This essay offers no opinion about Jackson's movie, except to observe that its multiple endings (if that is the right term for them) are a feature of Tolkien's book too. Indeed, the book has more end-matter than the movie because it contains a lengthy chapter, "The Scouring of the Shire," that did not find its way into the film. Of the nine chapters in

Book Six of *The Lord of the Rings*, two-thirds deal with events *following* the destruction of the Ring. After Gollum and the Precious have plunged into the Crack of Doom, Frodo states, "The Quest is achieved, and now all is over. I am glad you are here with me. Here at the end of all things, Sam." So concludes Chapter 3, "Mount Doom," but all is far from over at that point; we are only fifty-two pages in. A further eighty-five pages must elapse before we reach Sam's "Well, I'm back."

I make these observations not to imply any adverse judgement about the structure of Book Six but rather to raise a question about *The Lord of the Rings* as a whole: where does its rising action end and where does its falling action start? In other words, what is the narrative climax of Tolkien's epic and what constitutes the aftermath?

We will find an answer if we consult Tolkien's 1951 letter to Milton Waldman where he explains that "the story reaches its end (as a tale of Hobbits!) in the celebration of victory."[1] This celebration of victory occurs in a chapter entitled "The Field of Cormallen," the chapter that immediately follows the destruction of the Ring. It is this chapter that

[1] J.R.R. Tolkien to Milton Waldman (?Late 1951) in Wayne G. Hammond and Christina Scull, *The Lord of the Rings: A Reader's Companion* (London: HarperCollins, 2014), 748.

contains the story's "end," by the author's own reckoning. Or at least, it contains its end "as a tale of Hobbits," which allows for the fact that the story's end as a tale of Men (Aragorn's coronation, etc.) is yet to come.[2] Still, given that the story as a whole is chiefly about hobbits, and given that a large amount of activity awaits even them, this statement by Tolkien is instructive. He continues:

> In the scene where all the hosts of the West unite to do honour and praise to the two humble Hobbits, Frodo and Sam, we reach the 'eucatastrophe' of the whole romance: that is the sudden joyous 'turn' and fulfilment of hope, the opposite of tragedy, that should be the hallmark of a 'fairy-story' of higher or lower tone, the resolution and justification of all that has gone before. It brought tears to my eyes to write it, and still moves me, and I cannot help believing that it is a supreme moment of its kind.
>
> But it is not the end of the 'Sixth Book' or of *The Lord of the Rings* as a whole. For

---

[2] That the return of the king occurs *after* the end of the main story-line might seem perverse (given that the book is called *The Return of the King*) until we recall that the division into three volumes was made for publishing convenience, not because Tolkien had actually written a trilogy. If we keep in mind that *The Lord of the Rings* is one continuous story, the placement of Aragorn's coronation as part of the general "wrapping up" process may seem less eccentric.

> various reasons. The chief artistic one that the music cannot be cut off short at its peak. Also the history is left in the air, unfinished. Also I like tying up loose ends, and hate them in other people's books; I like to wind up the clues, as do not only children, but most folk of hearty appetite. Again, the story began in the simple Shire of the Hobbits, and it must end there, back to common life and earth (the ultimate foundation) again. Finally and cogently, it is the function of the longish *coda* to show the *cost* of victory (as always), and to show that no victory, even on a world-shaking scale, is final. The war will go on, taking other modes."[3]

According to Tolkien's own analysis here, the fulfilment of the whole romance, the "peak" of the story's music, is the scene where Frodo and Sam are praised at Cormallen. That is the climax of *The Lord of the Rings*. These "rejoicings at the Victory" mark the rising action's highest point.[4] Everything that comes after that scene, including even the coronation of Aragorn, comprises the coda — literally, the tail (Latin *cauda*). With "The Field of Cormallen" — the fifty-seventh of the story's sixty-

---

[3] Hammond and Scull, *A Reader's Companion,* 748.

[4] Ibid., 626.

two chapters — Tolkien concludes the body of the tale: then comes the tail of the body.

"The Field of Cormallen" is a chapter with many different facets, each of which helps to explain why Tolkien considered it the end of the hobbits' story. Perhaps its most striking aspect is its emotional tone, for the repeated mingling of laughter and tears bespeaks the eucatastrophic joy "poignant as grief" that Tolkien held to be a chief feature of this kind of story-telling.[5] Another prominent aspect is the rite of praise, for in such a logocentric world as Middle-earth it is not enough for Frodo and Sam heroically to bring about the Ring's destruction: their heroism must be celebrated by the minstrel of Gondor and general thanksgiving appropriately articulated. For this reason, Verlyn Flieger can say that "in one sense, the most important poem in the book is the Gondorian minstrel's lay" because it stands, within the fictive world, as the very first telling of the story that becomes *The Lord of the Rings*.[6] A third aspect we could consider is the presentation of Sam, for the action of the chapter is seen almost entirely from his perspective, indicating that he is assuming more

---

[5] J.R.R. Tolkien, *Tolkien On Fairy-stories*, ed. Verlyn Flieger and Douglas A. Anderson (London: HarperCollins, 2014), 75.

[6] Verlyn Flieger, *Interrupted Music: The Making of Tolkien's Mythology* (Kent, OH: Kent State University Press, 2005), 66.

and more the role of chief hero, as indeed Tolkien elsewhere designated him, while Frodo continues his gradual withdrawal from centre-stage, preparatory to his departure for the Grey Havens.[7]

These three aspects are among the reasons why "The Field of Cormallen" qualifies as the high point of the epic, but what this essay will focus on is something else, something less obvious, but something that may be all the more important *because* of its unobviousness. It is the chapter's topographical setting, Cormallen itself. As we will see, this Field, in Ithilien, is a place of tremendous significance, which deserves and will repay our closest attention.

The Field of Cormallen

We are told of the Field of Cormallen that it is "a wide green land and beyond it was a broad river in a silver haze, out of which rose a long wooded isle, and many ships lay by its shores. But on the field where they now stood a great host was drawn up, in ranks and companies glittering in the sun."[8] Later we learn

---

[7] J.R.R. Tolkien, *The Letters of J.R.R. Tolkien*, ed. Humphrey Carpenter (London: George Allen & Unwin, 1981), 161. Hereafter, *Letters*.

[8] J.R.R. Tolkien, *The Return of the King* (London: George Allen & Unwin, 1966), 231. Hereafter, *RK*.

more specifically that "The Field of Cormallen, where the host was now encamped, was near to Henneth Annûn [the Window on the West], and the stream that flowed from its falls could be heard in the night as it rushed down through its rocky gate, and passed through the flowery meads into the tides of Anduin by the Isle of Cair Andros." The trees surrounding the Field have "fluttering leaves" and after the celebrations are over and the glad day ends, "Frodo and Sam sat under the whispering trees amid the fragrance of fair Ithilien," talking deep into the night with their friends.[9]

It is a lovely setting, appropriate for the mood of peace and fulfilment that marks this episode. Still, what Tolkien gives the reader is only a brief sketch. One does not get the sense, either from the length of the description or its details, that a place of especially profound importance is being depicted. It is hardly surprising that the Field does not appear in Peter Jackson's movie, and whereas his omission of "The Scouring of the Shire" caused a great deal of consternation among admirers of the book, the absence of this scene went almost entirely unremarked.

---

[9] Tolkien, *RK*, 233.

Yet this is the setting Tolkien selects for the climactic celebrations, the scene that immediately precedes the coda of his epic. This is the place where the minstrel begs leave to sing of Frodo of the Nine Fingers and the Ring of Doom:

> And when Sam heard that he laughed aloud for sheer delight, and he stood up and cried: "O great glory and splendour! And all my wishes have come true!" And then he wept.
>
> And all the host laughed and wept, and in the midst of their merriment and tears the clear voice of the minstrel rose like silver and gold, and all men were hushed. And he sang to them, now in the Elven-tongue, now in the speech of the West, until their hearts, wounded with sweet words, overflowed, and their joy was like swords, and they passed in thought out to regions where pain and delight flow together and tears are the very wine of blessedness.[10]

In his letter to Waldman, as we saw above, Tolkien admitted that writing this passage brought tears to his eyes. In a letter to his aunt, Tolkien was more frank, disclosing that he didn't just well up, but actually wept: "I remember blotting the pages

---

[10] Tolkien, *RK*, 232.

(which now represent the welcome of Frodo and Sam on the Field of Cormallen) with tears as I wrote."[11] It is indeed a powerfully moving passage, and of great subsequent significance within the story itself, for, after the hobbits have returned to the Shire and Frodo has been treated with scorn by a ruffian, we are told that Pippin's thoughts "went back to the Field of Cormallen, and here was a squint-eyed rascal calling the Ring-bearer 'little cock-a-whoop'."[12] For Pippin, the public praise at Cormallen has become the touchstone of the respect that is now Frodo's due. Pippin does not think about Frodo's bearing of the Ring, nor even about the destruction of the Ring. The ceremony of thanksgiving is what sticks in his memory as the sign and seal of his friend's heroic achievement.

But why does Tolkien set that scene in this particular Field? Unless he has abandoned the basic canons of narrative art, such a climactic scene ought to be set in a place that resonates with and intensifies the significance of the action that it frames. King Lear rails against the storm while standing on a heath, not his hearth. Elizabeth Bennet awakens to Mr Darcy's true worth at

[11] Tolkien, *Letters*, 321.

[12] Tolkien, *RK*, 284.

Pemberley, not Netherfield. Plot and place comprise an integral whole, each intensifying the other, emotionally, morally, symbolically, thematically. A fundamental principle of fictional narration is that what happens and where it happens are meaningfully related.

Tolkien chooses to set the climax of his whole epic in a previously unvisited location. He has previously taken the reader to Ithilien, as we will discuss further below, but never before has he even mentioned the Field of Cormallen. Why not situate this episode in a place that has some pre-existing significance for the reader, such as Lothlórien or Rivendell? Admittedly, these places are a long way from Mount Doom, but there is no reason why the eagles could not have transported Frodo and Sam that far. The two hobbits have been asleep for about two weeks since they were "brought out of the fire."[13] The lengthy interval and the sleep indicate that Tolkien could have whisked the hobbits away to almost any destination he liked without needing to invent intermediate adventures that would have disrupted or prolonged the tale. It appears that he had originally expected to set the scene in Minas

---

[13] Tolkien, *RK*, 230.

Tirith, but when he came to write the chapter changed his mind.[14]

Evidently, the Field of Cormallen was not created *faute de mieux*. Tolkien invented this site for very definite purposes, and we will understand those purposes more fully if we examine the name "Cormallen."[15]

The philological origins of Middle-earth are well known. Tolkien himself readily acknowledged them, disclosing that his work was "*fundamentally linguistic* in inspiration" (his emphasis).[16] He goes on to say:

> The invention of languages is the foundation. The 'stories' were made rather to provide a world for the languages than the reverse. To me a name comes first and the story follows.[17]

---

[14] Christopher Tolkien reports that "There had been many mentions of a great feast to follow the final victory . . . but nothing had ever been said of it beyond the fact that it was to take place in Minas Tirith." J.R.R. Tolkien, *The History of Middle-earth, Vol. IX: Sauron Defeated*, ed. Christopher Tolkien (London: HarperCollins, 1992), 44. Hereafter, *HOME IX*.

[15] The name "Cormallen" (or "Kormallen" as it was originally spelled) appears to have been invented specifically for this chapter, though it did not appear in the very first draft. See *HOME IX*, 48-49.

[16] Tolkien, *Letters*, 219.

[17] Ibid.

If the name comes first, what does the name "Cormallen" mean? Fortunately, there is no doubt about that because Christopher Tolkien explains it in an Appendix to *The Silmarillion* entitled "Elements in Quenya and Sindarin Names." The definition provided there is highly suggestive, and we will unpack it slowly, taking it in three parts.

Trees

The Appendix to *The Silmarillion* reveals that the Field of Cormallen "was named from the *culumalda* trees that grew there."[18] This is the first thing to note about the field, that it is not just a large area of grass, but is home to a certain kind of tree, and we will turn our attention to that particular species — *culumalda* — in the second section of this analysis.

Trees in general are, of course, hugely important to Tolkien, who went so far as to call *The Lord of the Rings* "my own internal Tree."[19] As Dinah Hazell remarks in *The Plants of Middle-earth: Botany and Sub-creation*, "Trees have a central place in his creative imagination as well as in the plot, narrative technique, imagery, and mythology of *The Lord of*

---

[18] J.R.R. Tolkien, *The Silmarillion*, ed. Christopher Tolkien (London: HarperCollins, 2006), 333. Hereafter, *Silmarillion*.

[19] Tolkien, *Letters*, 321.

the Rings . . . individually and in forests, trees are essential to the atmosphere and action."[20] From the Party Tree to the White Tree of Gondor, from the *huorns* of the Old Forest to the *mallorns* of Lothlórien, from Old Man Willow to Treebeard and his fellow Ents, the whole sub-created world teems with arboreal characters and descriptions. Deep in the mythological background are the Two Trees of Valinor, Laurelin and Telperion, the great lamps that illumine day and night in Middle-earth.

Tolkien loved trees for their age, their beauty, their complexity. As a Christian, he would have seen in them a reflection of the cross of Christ, often figured in Scripture (and therefore in much sacred art and poetry) as a tree.[21] And as a philologist, he would have known that in Old English *treow* had several meanings: not only the obvious "tree," but also "truth" and "trust," and hence "fidelity" or "loyalty," as in the wedding vow, "I plight thee my troth." Hazell points out that the semantic overlap between "tree" and "trust" is a feature of many

[20] Dinah Hazell, *The Plants of Middle-earth: Botany and Sub-creation* (Kent, OH: Kent State University Press, 2006), 60-61.

[21] E.g., Acts 5:30; Galatians 3:13; 1 Peter 2:24.

languages, "based on the dependability and permanence of trees."[22]

"Cormallen," signifying a place where trees grow, is a name that reflects some of Tolkien's central aesthetic, religious, and moral preoccupations. Moreover, given its location in Ithilien, it is not just a field of trees but is located within a land of trees, for Ithilien as a whole is "a fair country of climbing woods."[23] We are first introduced to the region in *The Two Towers*, in the chapter entitled "Of Herbs and Stewed Rabbit":

> Many great trees grew there, planted long ago, falling into untended age amid a riot of careless descendants; and groves and thickets there were of tamarisk and pungent terebinth, of olive and of bay; and there were junipers and myrtles; and thymes that grew in bushes, or with their woody creeping stems mantled in deep tapestries the hidden stones; sages of many kinds putting forth blue flowers, or red, or pale green; and marjorams and new-sprouting parsleys, and many herbs of forms and scents beyond the garden-lore of Sam. The grots and rocky walls were already starred with saxifrages and

[22] Hazell, *Plants of Middle Earth*, 81.

[23] J.R.R. Tolkien, *The Two Towers* (London: George Allen & Unwin, 1966), 258. Hereafter, *TT*.

> stonecrops. Primeroles and anemones were awake in the filbert-brakes; and asphodel and many lily-flowers nodded their half-opened heads in the grass: deep green grass beside the pools, where falling streams halted in cool hollows on their journey down to Anduin.[24]

Hazell calls Ithilien "Tolkien's master achievement of woodland creation . . . The beauty of spring in the woods of Ithilien is depicted in a dense, brief space in the style of a medieval or epic catalog, overwhelming the reader and hobbits with a panoply of texture, color, and fragrance."[25] Gollum finds the fragrance choking, but the hobbits are refreshed and Sam laughs "for heart's ease not for jest."[26] As he rinses his gear after the feast of stewed coneys, Sam sees "the sun rise out of the reek, or haze, or dark shadow, or whatever it was, that lay ever to the east, and it sent its golden beams down upon the trees and glades about him."[27]

The sheer intensity and variety of the arboreal and floral descriptions here in Book Four is undoubtedly intended to establish Ithilien in the

---

[24] Tolkien, *TT*, 258.

[25] Hazell, *Plants of Middle Earth*, 49.

[26] Tolkien, *TT*, 259.

[27] Ibid., 264.

reader's mind as a place of rare beauty, the memory of which will make the return there all the more engaging when we reach it in Chapter 4 of Book Six. Almost all the trees and plants that the hobbits encounter in this earlier episode are, as Hazell observes, "prized as early heralds of the season [i.e., Spring] and for their aroma . . . And for Sam and Frodo, they bring the last bit of respite until they fulfil their Quest and return to Ithilien."[28] That this moment of respite occurs in Spring, and early Spring at that, is significant, and Tolkien is careful not to allow the story to get ahead of itself. In "Of Herbs and Stewed Rabbit" he strikes a delicate balance, gesturing towards the approach of a new season without prematurely realising it.[29] The word "already" shows that Spring has only just begun, while the words "desolate" and "dishevelled" restrain the overall mood, making it more promissory than actual. And this tentativeness is key to Tolkien's structural purposes: he must keep something back in order that the return to Ithilien, following the cataclysm on Mount Doom, will co-ordinate with the full arrival of Spring and all the expectant associations that accompany it. That the

[28] Hazell, *Plants of Middle Earth*, 50.

[29] Tolkien, *TT*, 258.

return occurs in April (on April 8th to be exact) rather than in Summer is highly significant and is something we will return to below.[30]

The return to Ithilien does not happen all in an instant; Tolkien introduces the new location with an initial note of doubt. When Sam awakes smelling a sweet air that reminds him of Ithilien's fragrance, he wonders how long he can have been asleep "for the scent had borne him back to the day when he had lit his little fire under the sunny bank; and for the moment all else between was out of waking memory."[31] Sam supposes that everything which seems to have occurred since he last smelled this air must have been only a dream. But then, when he sees Frodo's hand with the missing finger resting on the coverlet and realises that the intervening events actually happened, he concludes that he must have left the place. In which case, where is he? A voice assures him that he is truly "in the land of Ithilien."[32]

---

[30] Tolkien, *RK*, 376. As for reasons why this date might conceivably be significant to Tolkien, one possibility has to do with his school friend Vincent Trought, who was the first member of the TCBS to die, in 1912, after a long illness. Trought was born on 8th April 1893. For more on Trought, see John Garth, *Tolkien and the Great War: The Threshold of Middle-earth* (London: HarperCollins, 2003), 5, 6, 18, 19n, 28-9, 55.

[31] Tolkien, *RK*, 229.

[32] Tolkien, *RK*, 229.

Its sweet scent is not deceiving him; he has indeed returned to the "fair country of climbing woods." It is now time for him and Frodo to enter the very heart of this garden land and see that part of it which they had missed on their earlier visit, the place where the *culumalda* trees grow, the Field of Cormallen itself.

Golden Trees

The *culumalda*, according to Tolkien's unfinished Index to *The Lord of the Rings*, was "a tree with hanging yellow blossoms . . . growing in Ithilien espec[ially] at Cormallen."[33] The presence of these yellow-blossomed trees helps explain the etymology of "Cormallen," for the word *mal* means "gold" and is found in various terms, sometimes as a prefix, as in *Malinalda* ("Tree of Gold," another name for Laurelin) and *mallorn* (golden tree), and sometimes as an infix, as here in *Cormallen*.

If Tolkien loved trees in general, he had a special passion for golden trees, and we would do well to consider this fascination before focussing in on the particular kind of tree represented by the *culumalda*.

Outside of the Field of Cormallen, golden trees appear most notably in the Golden Wood, Lothlórien. Its original name, according to

[33] Hammond and Scull, *A Reader's Companion*, 626.

Treebeard, was *Laurelindórenan*: "That is what the Elves used to call it . . . Land of the Valley of Singing Gold."[34] Treebeard goes on to hum to himself, "*Laurelindórenan lindelorendor malinornélion ornemalin*," which Tolkien translates as follows: "*laure*, gold, not the metal but the colour, what we should call golden light; *ndor*, *nor*, land, country; *lin*, *lind-*, a musical sound; *malina*, yellow; *orne*, tree; *lor*, dream; *nan*, *nand-*, valley. So that roughly [Treebeard] means: 'The valley where the trees in a golden light sing musically, a land of music and dreams; there are yellow trees there, it is a tree-yellow land.'"[35]

The yellow or golden trees that chiefly grow in Lothlórien are *mallorns*. Sam is given a nut from one of these trees, which he plants back home in Hobbiton to replace the felled Party Tree: "a beautiful young sapling leaped up: it had silver bark and . . . burst into golden flowers in April."[36]

On the hobbits' return journey to the Shire, they stop off at Rivendell and tell Bilbo of their adventures. He struggles to understand what he has heard: "it is all so confusing . . . Aragorn's affairs, and

---

[34] Tolkien, *TT*, 70.

[35] Tolkien, *Letters,* 308.

[36] Tolkien, *RK*, 303.

the White Council, and Gondor, and the Horsemen, and Southrons, and oliphaunts . . . and caves and towers and golden trees, and goodness knows what besides."[37] The placement of "golden trees" last in this list of wonders seems significant, a nod, perhaps, to the culmination of the story "as a tale of Hobbits" in the Field of *culumalda*.

We have already noted how, in "Of Herbs and Stewed Rabbit," Sam watched the sun send "its golden beams down upon the trees and glades about him." When he finally enters Cormallen he discovers that the trees there are golden in reality, not just given an aurified appearance by the setting sun. Moreover, the *culumalda* are not fictional, without a referent or equivalent in the primary world, as the *mallorns* seem to be, but represent a particular species known to botanists. In his unfinished Index, Tolkien defines *Cormallen* as "a region in Ithilien (originally called after the laburnum that grew there)."[38]

Tolkien had had an interest in laburnums since at least his student days. We know this from his admiration for the work of the English Catholic poet

---

[37] Tolkien, *RK,* 265-266.

[38] Hammond and Scull, *A Reader's Companion,* 625.

Francis Thompson (1859–1907), an admiration that is worth exploring in some detail.

Thompson's poetry is now largely forgotten (except for "The Hound of Heaven," a poem about God's untiring pursuit of a human soul), but Tolkien knew it intimately. He owned the three-volume *Works of Francis Thompson* and gave a lecture to the Exeter College Essay Club while an undergraduate in which he described him as "among the very greatest of all poets."[39] The talk showed such knowledge of and sympathy for Thompson's work that the Club secretary recorded: "One was conscious that [Tolkien] has felt himself to be in perfect harmony with the poet."[40]

Raymond Edwards observes Thompson's interest in providing "unusually exact" botanical descriptions, along with an ability to introduce "theological themes and reflexions into quite disparate subjects."[41] In his talk at Exeter, Tolkien spoke of how Thompson combined things rational and mystical, emphasizing (so the Club secretary

---

[39] Quoted in Holly Ordway, *Tolkien's Modern Reading: Middle-earth Beyond the Middle Ages* (Park Ridge, IL: Word On Fire Academic, 2021), 231.

[40] Ibid.

[41] Raymond Edwards, *Tolkien* (London: Robert Hale, 2014), 43, 41.

minuted) "images drawn from astronomy and geology, and especially those that could be described as Catholic ritual writ large across the universe."[42] John Garth remarks, "It sounds like a foretaste of Middle-earth."[43] As Holly Ordway notes: "The attraction was evidently deep and strong."[44]

One particularly attractive work was the "Proem" from *Sister Songs*, in which the poet exclaims:

> Mark yonder, how the long laburnum drips
> Its jocund spilth of fire, its honey of wild
> flame!
> Yea, and myself put on swift quickening,
> And answer to the presence of a sudden
> Spring.[45]

The word *spilth* means "that which is spilled; the action or fact of spilling" (OED). It is an apt term, for the blossoms of the laburnum spill forth from its branches in such profusion that a mature healthy specimen appears to be a single large explosion of

---

[42] Quoted in Ordway, *Tolkien's Modern Reading,* 231.

[43] John Garth, *Tolkien at Exeter College* (Oxford: Exeter College, 2014), 30.

[44] Ordway, *Tolkien's Modern Reading,* 231.

[45] Francis Thompson, "Proem," *The Works of Francis Thompson. Poems: Volume I* (London: Burns & Oates, 1913), 26.

gold and yellow. The blossoms hang down in delicate pea-like clusters — "pendulous racemes," to give them their botanical name, — and that is why the tree is also known as Golden Chain or Golden Rain.[46]

Tolkien was so impressed by Thompson's arboreal depiction that it informed the way he created his own mythological tree, Laurelin ("Song of Gold"), whose fiery fruit was eventually formed into the Sun: "Flowers swung upon her branches in clusters of yellow flame, formed each to a glowing horn that spilled a golden rain upon the ground; and from the blossom of that tree there came forth warmth and a great light."[47] Tolkien writes of how the "spilth of Laurelin" is collected and kept "in great vats like shining lakes, that were to all the land of the Valar as wells of water and of light."[48] In a note on the typescript, he reveals that *spilth* is "meant to indicate that Laurelin is 'founded' on the laburnum. [From] 'jocund spilth of yellow fire' [by] Francis Thompson."[49]

---

[46] Walter S. Judd and Graham A. Judd, *Flora of Middle-earth: Plants of J.R.R. Tolkien's Legendarium* (New York: Oxford University Press, 2017), 203.

[47] Tolkien, *Silmarillion*, 26.

[48] Ibid., 27.

[49] J.R.R. Tolkien, *The History of Middle-earth, Vol. X: Morgoth's Ring*, ed. Christopher Tolkien (London: HarperCollins, 1993), 157-

This mythological background to Middle-earth, not to mention Thompson's influence upon it, may strike the average reader of *The Lord of the Rings* as esoteric and irrelevant, but we should note that Laurelin and her lunar partner, Telperion, are a living presence in the mind of Frodo. In *The Two Towers*, when torn over which way to go in order to fulfil his quest, Frodo reflects upon his "evil fate," a fate which he had taken on himself "in his own sitting-room in the far-off spring of another year, so remote now that it was like a chapter in a story of the world's youth, when the Trees of Silver and Gold were still in bloom."[50] The Two Trees of Valinor, though pre-historic from the Ring-bearer's vantage-point in time, have not been forgotten. Their significance lingers. The fact that one of those trees was a kind of laburnum is related to the fact that Frodo will eventually be praised, after the fulfilment of his quest, in a field of laburnums. It is no accident. The arboreal symmetry is integral to the structure of Tolkien's epic, a sign of its inner meaning, an indication that "a little halfling from the Shire, a simple hobbit of the quiet countryside," made the

158. Hereafter, *HOME X*. Tolkien slightly misquotes Thompson, inserting the adjective "yellow" into the cited phrase.

[50] Tolkien, *TT*, 252.

right choice at that crucial moment of decision.[51] He has achieved something of huge spiritual importance, has helped to maintain light amid the darkness. Frodo's heroism is rooted deep in the origin story of his own world and goes with the grain of Middle-earth.

If all that seems a bit grandiose, note how Tolkien has cleverly put the same tree before the reader in a playful, even comic, register long before Frodo ever set out on his journey, for laburnums have already appeared in Middle-earth in a much less grave context, as a description of Gandalf's fireworks. In *The Hobbit*, Bilbo praises his "laburnums of fire" that "hang in the twilight all evening."[52] Why laburnums and not some other specimen of golden flora, such as forsythia, acacia, or even daffodil or primrose? The fact that Tolkien specifies *laburnum* is deliberate. It is a little tell-tale sign of that tree's central place in his imagination. In the full flowering of his imagination, the laburnum will be shown to inform both Laurelin and the trees at Cormallen. We ought to be cognizant of these connections if we are to understand the full import

---

[51] Tolkien, *TT*, 252.

[52] J.R.R. Tolkien, *The Hobbit* (London: George Allen & Unwin, 1978), 14.

of the climactic scene. Cormallen is a field where trees grow, yes, but not any old trees: *golden* trees, laburnums, whose arboreal genealogy links them to the light of the world.

A Ring of Golden Trees

We now come to the pattern that these trees form, their arrangement in the Field of Cormallen. They are not positioned on one side only; they are not banked on opposite sides; they are not dotted around at random. They form a ring. The words "cor" and "corma" mean *ring* in Sindarin and Quenya respectively. As the Appendix to *The Silmarillion* reveals, "Cormallen" means *golden circle*.[53] Other key terms in the story show the same etymological root: Frodo and Sam are "cormacolindor" (*Ring bearers*); *Ringday*, the annual festival held to honour the completion of the Quest, is "Cormarë"; the Quenya title "i Túrin i Cormaron" means "the Lord of the Rings."[54] [55] [56]

---

[53] Tolkien, *Silmarillion*, 333.

[54] Tolkien, *RK*, 231, translated in *Letters*, 308.

[55] Ibid., 390.

[56] J.R.R. Tolkien to Philip Brown (30 May 1973). Quoted in Christina Scull and Wayne G. Hammond, *The J.R.R. Tolkien Companion and Guide: Chronology* (London: HarperCollins, 2017), 811.

The fact that Cormallen is so called for its *ring* of golden trees immediately suggests all sorts of interesting implications for the scene that takes place there. But before we reflect upon this circle of laburnums and think about possible purposes Tolkien had in mind as he created it, let us briefly survey his interest in rings and in gold more generally. Attention to his iconographical imagination as it bears upon these two things will help position us better to understand his intentions for the Field.

We noted above how, in *The Two Towers*, Tolkien introduces readers to the "fair country of climbing woods" that will reappear at the climax of his story. We ought now to notice that, in those earlier passages, Ithilien's flora is shown to have an ability to form itself in a circular fashion so as to cover up bad rings and to produce good rings.

In "Of Herbs and Stewed Rabbit," Sam, "smelling and touching the unfamiliar plants and trees," stumbles upon "a ring still scorched by fire, and in the midst of it he found a pile of charred and broken bones and skulls."[57] The ring in question is a patch of burnt earth and the fact that it contains scorched skeletons is an omen of the possible fate awaiting

[57] Tolkien, *TT*, 259.

Frodo and Sam in Mordor. However, it cannot withstand the fertility of Ithilien: "The swift growth of the wild with briar and eglantine and trailing clematis was already drawing a veil over this place of dreadful feast and slaughter."[58]

As well as being able to cover up an evil ring, the flora of Ithilien is shown to have the capacity for forming a good ring. At the Cross-roads, Frodo and Sam see a ruined stone figure, about whose "high stern forehead there was a coronal of silver and gold. A trailing plant with flowers like small white stars had bound itself across the brows as if in reverence for the fallen king, and in the crevices of his stony hair yellow stonecrop gleamed."[59] A "coronal" is a circlet or coronet, and this example, though "of silver and gold," is not made of metals, but is a natural wreath, formed out of white flowers and yellow stonecrop. It is a floral equivalent of Galadriel's name, which means "radiant garland," given because in her youth she had bound up her

[58] Tolkien, *TT*, 259.

[59] Ibid., 311.

hair "as a crown," golden but shot through with silver.[60 61 62]

There is a third natural ring to be found in Ithilien. The Cross-roads is situated in the middle of a wooded annulus, a "great ring of trees . . . a great roofless ring, open in the middle to the sombre sky . . . In the very centre four ways met."[63] Finding himself in the centre of something like a huge Celtic cross, the Ring-bearer must decide which course to take: "Reluctantly, Frodo turned his back on the West and followed as his guide led him, out into the darkness of the East. They left the ring of trees . . ."[64]

Leaving trees behind is never a good thing to do in Tolkien's world. It is an indication of the

---

[60] Tolkien, *Silmarillion*. 332.

[61] Tolkien, *Letters*, 428.

[62] The presence of gold *and* silver in Galadriel's hair, the coronal at the Cross-roads, the minstrel's voice, and the *mallorn* is intriguing and suggestive of the balance of influences descending from Laurelin and Telperion. In this connection we should note that Cormallen's circle of laburnums is located in *Ithilien*, a Sindarin name which means "Land of the Moon." The Field therefore provides yet another pairing of gold and silver, of Solar and Lunar significance. Read in religious terms, this pairing connotes the importance Tolkien attached not only to Christ ("the light of the world," John 8:12) but also to his mother, for the Blessed Virgin is often represented iconographically in Christian art by means of the Moon, which derives all its light from the Sun (see Revelation 12:1). For more on Tolkien's beliefs about Mary, see *Letters*, 172.

[63] Tolkien, *TT*, 310-311.

[64] Tolkien, *TT*, 312.

bleakness of the journey that awaits the hobbits, as the circularity not of wood but of metal — in the form of the One Ring — comes to dominate their experience more and more intensely.

From circles of trees (and other flora) we turn to circles of gold. There is not space here to discuss the "three rings for the Elven-kings," the "seven for the Dwarf-lords," and the "nine for Mortal Men." However, we must say something about the Ring of Power. As Gandalf explains to Frodo, Sauron made the One Ring himself and "let a great part of his own former power pass into it."[65] Sauron's power is thus concentrated into one particular golden object whereas the power of the other great evil figure in Middle-earth, Morgoth, is dispersed throughout gold in general and therefore is found in all things made of that metal. Tolkien explains:

> Sauron's power was not . . . in gold as such, but in a particular form or shape made of a particular portion of total gold. Morgoth's power was disseminated throughout Gold, if nowhere absolute (for he did not create Gold) it was nowhere absent. (It was this Morgoth-element in matter, indeed, which was a prerequisite for such 'magic' and other evils as Sauron

[65] J.R.R. Tolkien, *The Fellowship of the Ring* (London: George Allen & Unwin, 1966), 61. Hereafter, *FR*.

> practised with it and upon it.) It is quite possible, of course, that certain 'elements' or conditions of matter had attracted Morgoth's special attention . . . For example, all gold (in Middle-earth) seems to have had a specially 'evil' trend – but not silver.[66]

Given that gold in general is nowhere free of Morgoth's influence and given that rings of gold are particularly expressive of Sauron's power, we should note how Tolkien scatters various circles or bands of gold throughout the text, as an indication of the pervasiveness of evil, but also how he presents a number of more positive examples to suggest that evil does not have things all its own way.

Round the neck of the fallen Southron warrior is a "golden collar," suggestive of a slave's halter, and hence of the lies and threats that, so Sam wonders, may have led him to his death. The plaits of his hair are even "braided with gold" and there are "bands of gold" encircling the tusks of the oliphaunt, reflecting how minutely this controlling force extends among the Haradrim.[67]

---

[66] Tolkien, *HOME X*, 400.

[67] Tolkien, *TT*, 269-270.

Boromir's "belt of gold" is a more ambiguous example.[68] That it has been given to him by Galadriel implies that it is, in itself, innocent, and possibly therefore merely gold in colour, not made of golden metal (that distinction being important to Tolkien, as we saw above). But it is telling that she gives this gift to Boromir, rather than to any other member of the Fellowship. Is she signaling to Boromir that she perceives his morally compromised character? Or does she intend the gift to serve as a kind of inoculation against temptation, almost as if it were a kind of chastity belt, thus helping save Boromir from being permanently overtaken by the *libido dominandi* that besets him at the foot of Amon Hen? The way that Faramir takes special note of the belt when recounting his vision of his dead brother suggests the more positive interpretation.[69] Faramir reveals that Boromir was wearing not just a "belt of gold" — which is all we were told about it at the gift-giving scene in Lothlórien, — but bore "a fair belt, as it were of linked golden leaves, about his waist."

Interestingly, Goldberry, Tom Bombadil's wife, also wears a belt of gold. Goldberry, unlike Boromir, shows no sign of moral compromise, and this is

---

[68] Tolkien, *FR*, 391.

[69] Tolkien, *TT*, 274.

intimated by the fact that her belt is "shaped like a chain of flag-lilies set with the pale-blue eyes of forget-me-nots."[70] For Tolkien, with his deeply engrained Catholic sensibility, the lilies and the blueness would immediately connote purity by association with Marian iconography and therefore we should understand that Goldberry is immune from gold's corrupting power, just as her husband is immune from the Ring's ability to render its wearer invisible. Goldberry's very name, indeed, suggests that Sauron and Morgoth have not completely succeeded in colonising and corrupting all things round and gold.

And this reminds us that evil in Middle-earth is not ontologically equivalent with and opposite to goodness; the moral framework of Tolkien's world is not dualistic. Hence Elrond can say, "Nothing is evil in the beginning. Even Sauron was not so."[71] Likewise, Frodo can tell Faramir that Gollum is "not altogether wicked."[72] Tolkien informed a correspondent: "In my story I do not deal with Absolute Evil. I do not think there is such a thing, since that is Zero. I do not think that at any rate any

---

[70] Tolkien, *FR*, 134.

[71] Ibid., 281.

[72] Tolkien, *TT*, 301.

'rational being' is wholly evil."[73] The qualification there about "rational being" is important: Tolkien is covering his own back, for the story reveals (through the mouth of Elrond) that Sauron's Ring is indeed "altogether evil," which is why it cannot be redeemed and must be destroyed.[74] Stratford Caldecott argues that the circular shape of the Ring "is an image of the will closed in upon itself," its "empty centre" connoting the void that opens when "unseen by others, we are cut off from human contact, removed from the reach of friendship."[75] It is akin to the "hollow circle" on the Barrow-Downs: "in the midst of it there stood a single stone, standing tall . . . like a . . . guarding finger, or more like a warning."[76] The Ring in this sense is a functional equivalent of the evil hand that, in the teaching of Christ, must be amputated: "if your hand offend you, cut it off: it is better for you to enter into life maimed, than having two hands to go into hell, into the fire that never shall be quenched."[77] Frodo

[73] Tolkien, *Letters*, 243.

[74] Tolkien, *FR*, 281.

[75] Stratford Caldecott, *Secret Fire: The Spiritual Vision of J.R.R. Tolkien* (London: Darton, Longman & Todd, 2003), 60-61.

[76] Tolkien, *FR*, 148.

[77] Mark 9:43.

can only be liberated from this wholly evil thing when it is literally bitten off his body.

But rings (and hands) in general are not essentially or originally evil, any more than are Sauron and Morgoth. Tolkien, following Plotinus and St. Augustine, subscribes to a *privatio boni* theory of evil, which holds that evil has no substantial reality in itself, at least not at the rational level, although at the physical level evil may irremediably infect material things, which therefore have to be removed and incinerated. This was Tolkien's belief as a Christian and, given that *The Lord of the Rings* is, by his own description, "a fundamentally religious and Catholic work," we naturally see this ethical structure reflected in Middle-earth.[78] It has been created by the One, Eru Ilúvatar, and is therefore fundamentally good. Evil people and evil things are only corruptions or parodies of what they were originally and still ought to be.

It is therefore worth asking the question: of what is the One Ring a parody or distortion? At the moral level, the answer would be that the Ring parodies the power of Eru, twisting that creative and liberating energy into a destructive and coercive force. At the

---

[78] Tolkien, *Letters*, 172.

physical level, the answer is more complex: the Ring is a parody of anything that is innocently gold and circular. Such golden circles might be nothing more significant than a coronal of yellow stonecrop or a belt of linked leaves, — or even the bull's-eye in an archery target. ("Do I not hit near the mark?" asks Faramir. "Near," said Frodo, "but not in the gold.")[79] These various kinds of golden rings reveal that the One Ring has no monopoly on goldenness and circularity. Rather, the Ring is only a grossly, indeed maximally, distorted version of "the circles of the world."[80]

Which in turn prompts the question: where is the maximally *good* version of a golden ring in Middle-earth? And the answer to that must surely be, as this essay is attempting to show, the Field of Cormallen's circle of laburnums, given that it is here that the climax of the entire epic is set. The high point of the story naturally occurs in a place of the highest appropriateness. Here is the good ring, a ring of golden trees, the only such ring — apparently — in Middle-earth, the summit of its beauty. This ring encircles not the finger of a solitary and invisible power-addict, but a whole host of people gathered to

---

[79] Tolkien, *TT*, 277.

[80] Tolkien, *RK*, 343-344.

praise two hobbits for their heroism in having destroyed the prime tool of coercive force. Plot and place are mutually implicative; there is a meaningful relationship between what happens and where it happens.

Yet only if we know the etymology of "Cormallen" can we grasp this meaning. Why does Tolkien not make things more obvious? Why portray this crucial *mise-en-scène* in so understated a fashion? This is the final matter we have to consider.

All that is gold does not glitter

The etymology of "Cormallen" and its connection with laburnums are nowhere revealed in *The Lord of the Rings.* Tolkien makes it hard for his readers to pick up on the implications we have been exploring. And it is not just regular readers who, as a result, have missed the richness and aptness of the setting: scholars, too, have been surprisingly uninterested in what "Cormallen" means and why. Humphrey Carpenter omits the word from the index to his edition of Tolkien's letters, despite including entries for many much more obscure terms.[81] In *The Plants of Middle-earth*, Dinah Hazell makes not a

[81] Later editions of *Letters* contain an enlarged index compiled by Scull and Hammond in which "Cormallen" does appear.

single reference to laburnums, even though she rightly notes that "something as seemingly simple as a bloom can point to the inner life of a literary text."[82] In its entry for "Field of Cormallen," the Encyclopedia of Arda reports: "Given that Frodo the Ring-bearer was received here, it would be tempting to imagine that the field had been named in his honour: 'Cormallen the Field of the Golden Ring'. In fact, this connection seems to be entirely coincidental."[83] The Encyclopedia is correct that the Field has not been named in Frodo's honour and correct that his reception there is coincidental at the linguistic level, but the lack of further interest in this "coincidence" is remarkable. *The Lord of the Rings* is a work of artistic intelligence taken to extreme levels of detail, not a product of random irrational processes: there is no such thing in it as sheer coincidence.

It would appear that Tolkien has covered his tracks almost too well. The question then becomes: "Why work in this way? What end is served by burying the implications so deep?" Six answers present themselves for consideration.

---

[82] Hazell, *The Plants of Middle Earth*, 4.

[83] Mark Fisher, *The Encyclopedia of Arda: An Interactive Guide to the Works of J.R.R. Tolkien*. https://www.glyphweb.com/arda/c/cormallen.php

First, philology. Tolkien viewed the creation of Middle-earth as continuous with his academic interests in language. Writing *The Lord of the Rings* was not, he said, not "an aberration of an elderly professor of philology," nor was it "something quite different from one's work." Rather, it was "largely an essay in 'linguistic aesthetic', as I sometimes say to people who ask me 'what it is all about?'"[84] One feature of that linguistic aesthetic is linguistic archaeology: it is an essay in the importance of semantic origins. That the significance of the name "Cormallen" cannot be grasped except by careful attention to etymology provides a fictional analogue to (and indirect validation of) Tolkien's professional scholarship.

Second, freedom. Tolkien viewed *The Lord of the Rings* not as a work of allegory in which the author's purposes dominate, but as a work of "applicability," which "resides in the freedom of the reader."[85] If he had made the significance of Cormallen clearer, the story might have begun to look like a cipher with one set meaning. By keeping things unspecified, Tolkien leaves room for his readers to investigate connections or not, as they choose. It is an authorial

[84] Tolkien, *Letters*, 219-220.

[85] Tolkien, *FR*, 7.

strategy similar to the Socratic method of teaching, in which the mentor asks questions that provoke thought rather than dispensing answers that induce passivity; also to more contemporaneous "Easter eggs" in computer software and DVDs, where the creator deliberately leaves bonus features undocumented so that serendipitous discoveries can be made by their users.

Third, tone. Tolkien once remarked that, as a Christian, he did not expect the history of the primary world to be anything but a "long defeat," even though it may contain "some samples or glimpses of final victory."[86] The Third Age of Middle-earth has the same quality of gradual descent and transience, and if the implications of the scene at Cormallen, already a celebratory scene, had been made more plainly positive ("Here is the *good* Ring!"), the overall atmospheric balance would have been impaired. C.S. Lewis observed that a "profound melancholy" pervades the work and that "anguish" is "almost the prevailing note."[87] [88] The

---

[86] Tolkien, *Letters*, 255.

[87] C.S. Lewis, "The gods return to earth" [1954], *Image and Imagination: Essays and Reviews*, ed. Walter Hooper (Cambridge: Cambridge University Press, 2013), 102.

[88] C.S. Lewis to J.R.R. Tolkien (27 October 1949), *Collected Letters, Volume II*, ed. Walter Hooper (London: HarperCollins, 2004), 991.

reticence with which Tolkien sets out his stall here comports with that general tone.

Fourth, Englishness. Holly Ordway has helpfully pointed out that Tolkien had a typically English habit of understating what mattered to him most.[89] Though he could be hyperbolic about those things he rejected or denied, he tended to soft-pedal whatever he affirmed or claimed. Quite apart from the scholarly and artistic reasons he had for downplaying the significance of Cormallen, he had a native temperamental instinct for "covering" his top notes, as musicians say. To have made his meaning any more obvious would have been to risk inviting what to many English people still today, and especially to English *men* of Tolkien's generation and class, would have been the most disastrous of all epithets: "earnest."

Fifth, humility. One of the most admirable moral qualities of hobbits is their lack of self-importance. They are "unobtrusive," "fond of simple jests," interested more in food than themselves, and when in the days of Bilbo and Frodo they suddenly become "both important and renowned" it was "by no wish of their own."[90] Their motto was, in effect, "*nolo*

[89] Ordway, *Tolkien's Modern Reading,* 284-286.

[90] Tolkien, *FR*, 10-11.

heroizari," just as the motto of a priest should be "*nolo episcopari*."[91] In resting the Quest on their shoulders, Tolkien enacts his own belief that "we are all equal before the Great Author *qui deposuit potentes de sede et exaltavit humiles*."[92] Frodo, the humblest of the *humiles* and therefore "the best hobbit in the Shire," nevertheless fails in the Quest, finding himself unable to yield up the Ring at the last.[93] He only succeeds because of the pity he had earlier shown to Gollum: "He (and the Cause) were saved — by Mercy: by the supreme value and efficacy of Pity and forgiveness of injury."[94] In other words, the moment of truth that makes Frodo heroic passed him by at the time without his being aware of its significance. His own achievement is effectively invisible to him; he therefore blushes when he is praised at Cormallen. In the same spirit, Tolkien makes effectively invisible to the reader the inner meaning of that climactic scene. The mysteries of Providence are on display, and a

---

[91] Tolkien, *Letters*, 215. "I do not want to be a hero," "I do not want to be a bishop."

[92] Ibid. The Great Author is God, "who puts down the mighty from their throne and exalts the humble" (Luke 1:52).

[93] Tolkien, *FR*, 151.

[94] Tolkien, *Letters* 251-252.

mystery, if it is to be depicted accurately, must by definition be unobvious.

Sixth, latency. We here return to the point made above about the Cormallen scene being set in early April, for the timing is foundational to the scene's unobviousness. Laburnums flower in May, not April.[95] Frodo and Sam are praised amid a circle of trees that are only beginning to bud with golden blooms; their full glory is yet to be revealed. Tolkien paid minute attention to the chronology of his story (ensuring, for instance, that all the phases of the Moon were consistent) and cannot have been unaware of the botanical calendar as it pertained to the laburnums. His decision to date the Cormallen scene to Spring, not Summer, may be explained in part by four of the five reasons already given in this section: freedom, tone, Englishness, and humility. But it is worth specifying latency as a separate, sixth reason, because latency is an essential feature of Middle-earth.

"All that is gold does not glitter," as Gandalf writes of Aragorn, who, early in the story, has travelled under the name Strider, using "many

---

[95] Laburnums are known in Italian as *maggiociondolo* ("May-pendant") and given that the Field of Cormallen is near Cair Andros, about fifty miles north of Minas Tirith, which Tolkien said was on "about a latitude of Ravenna," this Italian name is not irrelevant. (Quoted in Ordway, *Tolkien's Modern Reading*, 178.)

disguises" so as to "hide his true shape."[96] [97] Frodo demonstrates perceptiveness when he says to this unknown Ranger, "I think you are not really as you choose to look."[98] Over time, of course, Aragorn's identity is revealed, both to himself and to others, as he comes into his own.

The ability to see beyond appearances is crucial in Middle-earth as it was crucial for Tolkien in the primary world. As a Christian, Tolkien's religious life was centred on the Blessed Sacrament: "Not for me the Hound of Heaven [Francis Thompson again!], but the never-ceasing silent appeal of Tabernacle."[99] The Tabernacle is the place in a Catholic church where the Blessed Sacrament is reserved as a focus for prayer and devotion and in readiness for the next celebration of Mass. While the Sacrament is locked in the Tabernacle it cannot be seen or tasted or touched; nonetheless, it is sacred, so Tolkien believed, and worshippers genuflect before it. At services of Benediction, Tolkien would have sung innumerable times the eucharistic hymn of St Thomas Aquinas: "Adoro te devote, latens Deitas /

[96] Tolkien, *FR*, 182.

[97] Tolkien, *RK*, 341.

[98] Tolkien, *FR*, 178.

[99] Tolkien, *Letters*, 340.

Quae sub his figuris vere latitas" ("I adore Thee devoutly, hidden God, / Thou who hidest truly in these shapes"). Similarly, albeit not allegorically, within Middle-earth Gandalf is a servant of "the Secret Fire," the Flame Imperishable that burns "at the heart of the world."[100] Unless we are attuned to the secret qualities in Tolkien's sub-created world, we will be missing half the picture; much of its true nature is hidden because hiddenness is in the nature of the deepest realities. The beauty of this golden ring of trees does not mean it must be portrayed in full Summer-time obviousness. Immediate sensory data are not the ultimate factors in perception. Seeing with the mind and heart is more decisive than seeing with the eye. On the Field of Cormallen we are shown "ranks and companies glittering in the sun" but the laburnums are not shown glittering with golden flowers. "All that is gold does not glitter." The trees will come into their glory in due time, but only after the hobbits have left and once Summer has arrived. The start of Summer is May Day, the date on which Aragorn will be crowned king, and the date which, one year hence, will mark Sam's wedding to Rosie. Every Summer the circle of trees will show its goldenness. Remembering that

[100] Tolkien, *FR*, 344, Tolkien, *Silmarillion*, 13.

fact and acknowledging its significance is immeasurably more important than witnessing it first-hand. To put it in religious terms: "Blessed are those who believe without having seen."[101]

Conclusion

We have examined six possible reasons why Tolkien depicted the Field of Cormallen in such an understated fashion despite its importance as the site of the story's climactic scene. The number six, however, is not a number on which to end; we must say one more thing, following the example of Tolkien himself, who often selected the number seven when he wished to portray completion.[102]

It is symbolically and sinisterly apt that Frodo puts on the ring a total of six times: in Tom Bombadil's house, at The Prancing Pony, on Weathertop, twice on Amon Hen, and lastly on Mount Doom. In Biblical numerology six symbolizes evil because it falls just short of the perfect seven. 666 is the pre-eminently evil number ("the number of the Beast") because it falls short of seven three

[101] John 20:29.

[102] Sam is elected Mayor of the Shire seven times (*RK* 378). Aragorn is "nine and forty years of age" (i.e., 7 x 7) when Arwen sees him "under the trees of Caras Galadhon laden with flower of gold" and "her choice was made and her doom appointed" (*RK* 341).

times over; it is a blasphemous parody of the Holy Trinity.[103]

Is it too fanciful to suggest that, when he walks into the circle of laburnums at Cormallen, Frodo "puts on the ring" — so to speak — a seventh time, except that this time it is the good ring, the true ring, of which Sauron's ring was but a parody? Frodo now has only nine fingers and could not wear the Precious even if he wanted to. The finger on the hand that offended him has been cut off by Gollum's teeth and cast away to be burnt. But as a result of that loss, Frodo has been freed to have his whole being surrounded by beauty and life and fragrance, by "jocund spilth of yellow fire."

Be that as it may, Frodo and Sam between them certainly lose one ring and find another. What they helped destroy was inert and hollow, addictive and treacherous. What they enjoy as a result is a ring of golden trees, ready to spill forth light upon a Field in Ithilien at the May-time return of the king.

---

[103] Revelation 13:18.

A Passage to Something Better

Annie Nardone on Tolkien's Approach to Virtue

> He [Tolkien] folded into his work something fresh and unexpected, something vital and important: a tear drop from his own flesh and blood. From one perspective, the change was minor, almost negligible, but from another, it made a world of difference.
>
> — Holly Ordway, *Tolkien's Modern Reading*[1]

Perhaps it is an easy path to tread when devotees of J.R.R. Tolkien's *Lord of the Rings* repeatedly credit his medieval studies as his primary inspiration. Dr. Holly Ordway makes a key point regarding the true span of literary influence directing Tolkien's writing in her thoroughly academic and delightfully accessible text *Tolkien's Modern Reading*. She writes that "Yes, Tolkien was, above all things, a

---

[1] Holly Ordway, *Tolkien's Modern Reading* (Park Ridge, IL: Word on Fire, 2021), 292.

medievalist" but proves that "his modern reading was both more far-reaching than people have realized, and more significant for his creative imagination than has been assumed."[2] Her research clearly supports the fact that the scope of Tolkien's reading enabled him to approach themes like death, loyalty, and bravery in a manner that speaks well to the 21st century mind.

For example, on the subject of heroism and death, which are core themes in medieval literature, author William Morris's influence on Tolkien's heroic character development is evident in the character of the shieldmaiden, Èowyn. Ordway writes,

> Interestingly, Tolkien heightens the importance of Èowyn's role. Unlike Hall-Sun, Eowyn is explicitly and publicly assigned the role of homestead guardian because of her courage and spirit: "She is fearless and high-hearted. All love her. Let her be as lord to the Eorlingas, while we are gone," says Hama. "It shall be so." Theoden declares, and so it is. Èowyn is affirmed not only by the non-warriors left behind but by the warriors themselves; indeed, she is named as a leader in much the same way that Thiodolf himself, in

[2] Ordway, *Tolkien's Modern Reading*, 292.

> The House of the Wolfings, is chosen as head of the war-band by popular acclaim. In this way, Tolkien gives Èowyn a role similar to, but considerably more significant than, that of her Morrisian precursor.[3]

As Ordway notes, the subject of death in Tolkien's legendarium is connected to ancient as well as modern writing influences.

We moderns are uncomfortable with death; rather than engaging with our mortality, society looks away from the inevitable. J.R.R. Tolkien approaches the subject of death with truth and grace, confronting the subject and what lies beyond:

> *But I might say that if the tale is 'about' anything (other than itself), it is not as seems widely supposed about 'power'. Power-seeking is only the motive-power that sets events going, and is relatively unimportant, I think. It is mainly concerned with Death, and Immortality; and the 'escapes': serial longevity, and hoarding memory.*[4]

---

[3] Ordway, *Tolkien's Modern Reading*, 172.

[4] J.R.R. Tolkien, *The Letters of J.R.R. Tolkien*, ed. Humphrey Carpenter and Christopher Tolkien (New York: Houghton Mifflin Harcourt, 2000), 284.

> *Here are beauties which pierce like swords or burn like cold iron; here is a book that will break your heart.*[5]
>
> — *C.S. Lewis, Image and Imagination*

Tolkien, commenting on *The Lord of the Rings* in a letter of 14th October, 1958, stated that "It [*Lord of the Rings*] is mainly concerned with Death, and Immortality." This theme is the warp upon which the story is woven. In fact, death in some manner appears subtly in many chapters; symbolically as a shadow or as a change of heart, physical death as a noble act, or a natural conclusion of life on earth that moves to immortal life. For the living, death is a pathway or a purpose, not an end. Tolkien writes from his Christian view, portraying death as a symbolic and noble passage and as a gateway to the hope of immortality. Death is necessary, not something to be reviled or feared.

A personality transition can be a symbolic death. Faramir and Èowyn are recovering after battle in the Houses of Healing. Faramir has fallen in love with this shieldmaiden of Rohan. When he asks for her love in return, she answers, "I wished to be loved by

[5] C.S. Lewis, *Image and Imagination* (New York: HarperCollins, 2014), 100, Digital Edition.

another. But I desire no man's pity."[6] Faramir knows that she "desired to have the love of the Lord Aragorn . . . But when he gave you only understanding and pity, then you desired to have nothing, unless a brave death in battle.'"[7] The shadow of discontent over her mind is like a living death that she cannot shake. The only resolution that she sees as a cure is not to rest in the Houses of Healing, but a noble death in war. She "looked for death in battle. But I have not died, and battle still goes on" — not just for Middle Earth, but also for Èowyn's mind and heart.[8] She declares, "I do not desire healing. I wish to ride to war . . . like Théoden the king, for he died and has both honour and peace."[9] She believes that her only escape from the living death that traps her is a noble physical death in battle. Dying to our selfish desires requires a conscious decision and this proves difficult for the strong-minded Éowyn.

Faramir assures her that she already possesses what she desires to die for. He does not pity her, but

---

[6] J.R.R. Tolkien, *The Return of the King* (New York: Houghton Mifflin Harcourt, 1994), 943.

[7] Ibid.

[8] Ibid., 938.

[9] Ibid., 939.

tells her, "For you are a lady high and valiant and have yourself won renown that shall not be forgotten."[10] What stands before her is the real fulfillment of her wishes — her true destiny, not the hollow desires based on pride that she believes in. "Then the heart of Èowyn changed, or at last she understood it. And suddenly her winter passed, and the sun shone on her."[11] Èowyn laid down her dark "shield" forged of pride, defiance, and unrequited love to step into the light of her destiny. She transitioned from a war-like, masculine personality to a healing feminine nature. She tells Faramir "Behold! The Shadow has departed! I will be a shieldmaiden no longer, nor vie with the great Riders, nor take joy only in the songs of slaying. I will be a healer and love all things that grow and are not barren."[12] Èowyn now rejoices in restoring life rather than death. Likewise, when we finally reconcile ourselves with our true purpose, we find peace.

Faramir's transformation also presents a symbolic death. He transforms from a servant who lives in the shadow of his brother, Boromir, to

---

[10] Tolkien, *The Return of the King,* 943.

[11] Ibid., 943.

[12] Ibid.

becoming Steward of the Realm of Gondor. His father, Denethor, commands Faramir to lead perilous charges that should end with certain death. He constantly reminds Faramir of Boromir's battle successes and Faramir's failures. People murmur, "They give him no rest. The Lord [Denethor] drives his son too hard, and now he must do the duty of two, for himself and for the one that will not return."[13] Humble and obedient, Faramir tells Denethor, "Since you are robbed of Boromir, I will go and do what I can in his stead — if you command it."[14] At Denethor's edict, Faramir nearly dies in a hopeless battle at Osgiliath. Prince Imrahil brings the wounded Faramir to the White Tower, but Denethor, under the dark influence of Sauron, tries to burn them both alive on a pyre and end the Steward's reign on his terms. Denethor perishes, but Faramir is rescued, healed and becomes the noble Steward of the Realm in his stead. One may wonder why Tolkien wrote of a violent death for Denethor; we are all given an opportunity to choose between humility or pride, repentance or evil. We see that the pride of one person and one decision can potentially bring down an entire kingdom. Denethor's mad

---

[13] Tolkien, *The Return of the King*, 798.

[14] Ibid.

choice sets in motion the death of the decaying order of Gondor and its rebirth with Faramir as Steward.

The House of Gondor experiences a symbolic death and rebirth. Gimli and Legolas enter the city after the battle of the Pelennor Fields. Gimli studies the walls of the city and comments on "some good stone-work here."[15] But Legolas observes, "They need more gardens. The houses are dead, and there is too little here that grows and is glad. If Aragorn comes into his own the people of the Wood shall bring him birds that sing and trees that do not die."[16] When the citizens return to Gondor, they are "laden with flowers" and play all manner of instruments with the "clear-voiced singers," bringing music, the "language of creation."[17] [18] [19] Only growing things can bring life to cold stone.

The physical death and redemption of one member of the Fellowship early in the adventure is poignant because of its depiction of deceit, forgiveness, and sacrifice. Boromir attacks Frodo in

---

[15] Tolkien, *The Return of the King*, 854.

[16] Ibid.

[17] Ibid., 944.

[18] Ibid.

[19] Peter Kreeft, "The Lord of the Rings: Beauty and Language," *YouTube*, accessed December 10, 2018, https://youtu.be/Tku1r7tFE6I.

his attempt to steal the ring for his father, Denethor, claiming that he only wants to borrow it. When Frodo refuses, Boromir accuses him of "running willfully to death and ruining our cause!"[20] But it is Boromir who has started down the path to his own death. He then feels convicted about what he has done and "for a while he was as still as if his own curse had struck him down" Boromir's guilt leaves him helpless to explain what came over him.[21] When Aragorn finds him after battle, the dying Boromir confesses for absolution. Aragon blesses and assures him that Minas Tirith and his people will not fall. This scene bears a similarity to Adam as he is questioned by God in the Garden. He blames, confesses, but brings death upon himself. Boromir's sin has led to his death, but he also met with forgiveness. His mistakes lead to the Fellowship's splintering, a move that was ultimately beneficial toward the final victory over Sauron. Even events that seem dire can be part of a grander plan for good.

Théoden endured not only a symbolic, nearly spiritual death and renewal but also a physical death with a glimpse into immortality. When Aragorn, Gimli, Legolas, and Gandalf come to Edoras to speak

---

[20] Tolkien, *The Return of the King*, 390.

[21] Ibid.

with Théoden, they are met with a cold reception. Deceit and evil had already established a stronghold there through the treachery of Saruman and in the figure of Gríma Wormtongue. Gandalf calls him a "snake" and that image of the snake in the Garden of Eden describes Gríma perfectly.[22] As the snake whispered half-truths to Adam to bend his will to evil, Gríma's words slowly destroyed the once noble king — all directed toward the dismantling of the goodness in Middle-earth. Aragorn and company walk into the hall and find not a king, but instead "a man so bent with age that he seemed almost a dwarf."[23] A glimmer of the former mind could be seen in his eyes that "still burned with a bright light, glinting as he gazed at the strangers."[24] Evil brings destruction and death. The great king has 'died' and the husk of an old man remains.

Not content to only twist Théoden's mind, Wormtongue weaves in subterfuge about Gandalf and the others in the presence of the court, claiming that they are working "in league with the Sorceress of the Golden Wood."[25] Gandalf, who has "passed

---

[22] Tolkien, *The Return of the King*, 509.

[23] Ibid., 501.

[24] Ibid.

[25] Ibid., 502.

through fire and death" in his battle with the Balrog, raises his staff and lifts the curse that has influenced Théoden's mind, telling him, "Too long have you sat in shadows and trusted to twisted tales and crooked promptings."[26] [27] Gandalf resurrects Theoden to his former strength, telling him to "look out upon your land. Breathe the free air again!"[28] His mind cleared by goodness and truth, he stands noble once again, brought back from a symbolic death.

Théoden experiences physical death but holds to a beautiful faith of a continuing life beyond death. Tolkien now gives us a vision of the restored King. He has rallied the Riders of the Mark, and Merry joins them in preparation for battle. Théoden's bent figure springs up,

> tall and proud he seemed again; and rising in his stirrups he cried in a loud voice, more clear than any there had ever heard a *mortal* man achieve before . . . "Ride now, ride now! Ride to Gondor!" . . . Fey he seemed, or the battle-fury of his fathers ran like new fire in his veins, and he was borne up on Snowmane like a god of old, even as Oromë the Great in the battle of

---

[26] Tolkien, *The Return of the King*, 503.

[27] Ibid.

[28] Ibid., 504.

> the Valar when the world was young. His golden shield was uncovered, and lo! It shone like an image of the Sun.[29]

Tolkien's vivid imagery depicts a king and leader who was battle-ready and glorious, resurrected from rot — a stark contrast to the withered old man found by Gandalf.

On the Pelennor Fields, Théoden lies wounded and near death and at the mercy of the Dark Lord of the Nazgul. It seems that darkness has finally won. But as Merry looks at him, the King opens his eyes and bids Merry farewell, saying, "My body is broken. I go to my fathers. And even in their mighty company I shall not now be ashamed . . . a grim morn, a glad day, and a golden sunset!"[30] As he lay dying, he motions for the banner to be passed to Éomer, the new king and tells them "Hail, King of the Mark! Ride now to victory!"[31] Théoden passes, not in fear of the unknown or darkness of the end, but with anticipation to join the spiritual realm of the past kings for eternity.

The story's thread of life, near-death, and immortality is clearly depicted by Frodo, the brave

---

[29] Tolkien, *The Return of the King*, 820.

[30] Ibid., 824.

[31] Ibid., 825.

"Ring-bearer" hobbit. Frodo nearly dies many times on his journey to destroy the Ring in Mount Doom. One night early in the adventure, the hobbits and Strider were encamped on Weathertop where Frodo was attacked and stabbed by a Wraith. Like a cry of fervent prayer, he exclaimed, "O Elbereth! Gilthoniel!" and the five Wraiths disappeared.[32] But the damage was done. Frodo's near-deadly wound to his shoulder was a physical curse he carried until his final voyage to the Grey Havens. Strider assures Sam that Frodo isn't dead — shouting the name of Elbereth was a dangerous spell against the Wraiths. Frodo remembered the names Elbereth and Gilthoniel from long ago when he left Hobbiton and heard the High Elves singing "Gilthoniel! O Elbereth! / Clear are thy eyes and bright thy breath! / Snow-white! Snow-white! We sing to thee / In a far land beyond the sea."[33] The sound and melody "seemed to shape itself in their thought into words which they only partly understood."[34] But at that critical moment, Frodo was compelled to call out the name of the star-queen when he was set for death at the hand of the Wraith. The knowledge that Frodo

---

[32] Tolkien, *The Return of the King*, 191.

[33] Tolkien, *The Fellowship of the Ring*, 78.

[34] Ibid.

needed to survive the attack was learned long before he needed it or understood the words. God intervenes in our own lives to provide us with experiences and memories to be hidden away in our minds, preparing us for future hardships.

Frodo's next brush with death is his encounter with the monstrous spider, Shelob. Accompanied by his ever-faithful Sam, they are lured into the spider's lair by Gollum's deceitful trickery. Frodo is stung, bound, and put into a deathlike trance by the spider. A long-buried memory of the elves comes to Sam's mind and he calls out to Galadriel when he finds the Phial of Light that she gave to Frodo. This time, it is Sam who sings out the same names that Frodo exclaimed on Weathertop, invoking the help of "Gilthoniel A Elbereth!"[35] He begins to sing the music of the Elves, a language he does not know, but remembers hearing in the house of Elrond. At first, Sam believes for certain that Frodo is dead, until he holds the Light of Galadriel over him and sees that "Frodo's face was fair of hue again, pale but beautiful with an elvish beauty."[36] The sight of Frodo gives him "bitter comfort" and a hope to continue with the

---

[35] Tolkien, *The Two Towers*, 712.

[36] Ibid., 716.

mission.[37] Unsure if Frodo dies at this point, Sam takes the Ring on the chain and resolves to complete its destruction. Again, we see that the wisdom we are given throughout our lives can save us. Sam and Frodo never considered that Elven song as important to their journey, but Tolkien shows the reader that there is no experience wasted in life, and death is not the end if there is purpose in it.

At the conclusion of *Return of the King*, Frodo, Sam, Pippin, and Merry return to the Shire to live. Life has returned to a somewhat normal pace, with token pieces of the past still evident. Merry and Pippin wear their mail-shirts and tell tales, Sam falls in love and marries, but Frodo is restless. His old injuries from the Wraith and Shelob pain him and on the anniversary of receiving the stab wound on Weathertop, Frodo grows "very pale and his eyes seemed to see things far away."[38] He feels the ache and longing for something else that the Shire cannot give. He tells Sam, "I am wounded; it will never really heal."[39] So after two years, Frodo decides that it is time to take the opportunity to gather his papers and writings, especially the "big book with plain red

[37] Tolkien, *The Two Towers*, 716.

[38] Tolkien, *The Return of the King*, 1002.

[39] Ibid.

leather covers; its tall pages were now almost filled" with wisdom gathered, the history of Bilbo's experiences and the story of the Fellowship's quest.[40] Sam remarks that it was nearly finished, but Frodo explains that as his part in the story comes to an end, Sam's begins. Thus, Frodo leaves his story, added to Bilbo's, for the next generations, providing a timeline for Sam to continue. This written story, like a great epic or the Bible narrative, shows purpose in the good and bad events in life and how they play a part in a grander plan. Bilbo and the Fellowship may not have understood the purpose in an isolated tragedy like Boromir's death, but in the broad sweep of their history, events begin to fit together.

As they journey to the boat that will take Frodo to the Grey Havens, Sam hears Frodo singing the old walking song, but he has changed the words slightly. The last line has a finality to it. Rather than "And take the hidden paths that run / Towards the Moon or to the Sun," Frodo sings softly to himself, "Shall take the hidden paths that run / West of the Moon, East of the Sun."[41] The destination of this final journey will go past what they know, to a place

---

[40] Tolkien, *The Return of the King*, 1003.

[41] Ibid., 1005.

beyond "the grey rain-curtain turned all to silver glass." Frodo will see "white shores and beyond them a far green country under a swift sunrise."[42] He is on his way to what lies beyond our world and the mortal life, to something better that promises rest and release to something, or some place, better and lasting.

The Lady Galadriel and Elrond, who lived several lifetimes, choose to diminish into the West because their work in Middle Earth was completed. There must be an end to living to begin the next life. As Sam watched the boat sail away across the grey sea, "he saw only a shadow on the waters that was soon lost in the West."[43] He couldn't see anything beyond his world because it was not his time to leave. Sam still has a purpose in the Shire.

Frodo tells Sam, "I tried to save the Shire, and it has been saved, but not for me. It must often be so, Sam, when things are in danger: someone has to give them up, lose them, so that others may keep them."[44] Dear, brave Sam is now at the helm. Merry and Pippin are once again blessing the Shire with their joy and storytelling. Their perilous journey

---

[42] Tolkien, *The Return of the King*, 1007.

[43] Ibid.

[44] Ibid., 1006.

gave them the courage and knowledge they needed to build up the Shire. When our "age" ends, we will also pass away, but as we read about the departure of Frodo to the Grey Havens, we must inspire others who can step in to carry on for us, and then we will, like Frodo, see the "grey rain-curtain turned all to silver glass" and we will behold the "white shores and beyond them a far green, country under a swift sunrise."[45]

Like Frodo, we are inevitably brought to our own Grey Havens — heaven — as a forever cessation from the difficulties that we experience in life. Passage to an eternal, heavenly home as depicted by the Grey Havens should be sweetly anticipated. Death is not the end, just a gateway to a new realm where we join the loved ones who have gone before us. Tolkien's storytelling about redemption, death, and eternity in *The Lord of the Rings* can encourage the believer, reminding us that there is something beyond what we can physically see. It can also challenge the seeker to think, "What if there is an ending to this life that is even better than anything we could experience here?"

Tolkien stated in his letter to Miss Rhona Beare, 14 October, 1958, that *The Lord of the Rings* "is

[45] Tolkien, *The Return of the King,* 1007.

mainly concerned with Death, and Immortality."[46] Indeed, the epic is rife with symbolic and physical death and near-death with recovery. Immortality can be gained by renown that is written and retold in stories, or like Théoden who joins the past Kings of Rohan after he dies. Frodo, Bilbo, Gandalf, and the Elves leave Middle Earth because "the Third Age was over, and the Days of the Rings were passed and an end was come of the story and song of those times."[47] Frodo, Bilbo, and Gandalf are older, weary, and their legacy with the ring is complete. The heroes of the story who died never feared death because they knew that something better waited for them. As Tolkien read through *The Lord of the Rings*, he "became aware of the dominance of the theme of Death."[48] He writes in a letter, dated 10 April 1958, "But certainly Death is not an Enemy!"[49] This epic tale encourages us to face our eventual mortal end with hope — the trust in a high calling and an eternal home.

---

[46] J.R.R. Tolkien, *The Letters of J.R.R. Tolkien*, ed. Humphrey Carpenter and Christopher Tolkien (New York: Houghton Mifflin Harcourt, 2000), 284.

[47] Tolkien, *The Return of the King*, 1006.

[48] Tolkien, *The Letters of J.R.R. Tolkien*, 267.

[49] Ibid.

Gandalf: The Prophetic Mentor

Zak Schmoll on the Defeat of Sauron

Near the beginning of the Third Age of Middle-earth, the Valar commissioned the Istari as representatives from the Maiar to resist Sauron's rise. Of the five chosen, only Olórin, better known as Gandalf, remained true to his mission until the end. As he tells the newly enthroned Aragorn, "The Third Age was my age. I was the Enemy of Sauron; and my work is finished."[1] His opposition to Sauron is publicly displayed while standing outside the walls of Minas Tirith or at the Black Gate. On the battlefield, he drew his sword to strike down the servants of the enemy, but Gandalf's most significant strike to the enemy happened prior to these final battles. This essay will explore Gandalf as a prophetic mentor who defeated Sauron long before

---

[1] J.R.R. Tolkien, *The Lord of the Rings* (New York: Houghton Mifflin Harcourt, 2002), 971.

the actual downfall of Barad-dûr by guiding Hobbits in the ways of pity.

The many names of Gandalf will be utilized throughout this essay interchangeably, and they can be found in a memory Faramir shares with Frodo. "Many are my names in many countries, he said. Mithrandir among the Elves, Tharkûn to the Dwarves; Olórin I was in my youth in the West that is forgotten, in the South Incánus, in the North Gandalf; to the East I go not."[2]

Little is said about Olórin in *The Silmarillion*, but the reader is given a small glimpse into his character. He is described as being the "wisest" Maiar who put "fair visions or the promptings of wisdom" into the hearts of the Elves in Lorien.[3] He is also described as spending a great good time with the Valar Nienna, "and of her he learned pity and patience."[4] Nienna's position among the Valar is unique as she lived alone and "is acquainted with grief, and mourns for every wound that Arda has suffered in the marring of Melkor . . . But she does not weep for herself; and those who hearken to her learn

---

[2] Tolkien, *The Lord of the Rings*, 670.

[3] J.R.R. Tolkien, *The Silmarillion*, ed. Christopher Tolkien (New York: Houghton Mifflin Harcourt, 1977), 18.

[4] Ibid.

pity, and endurance in hope."[5] Even before he comes to Middle-earth as Gandalf, he is already cultivating the value of pity within himself.

Pity becomes such an essential characteristic of Gandalf that he tells Frodo that if he were to succumb to the Ring's power, it would be through pity. He says, "Yet the way of the Ring to my heart is by pity, pity for weakness and the desire of strength to do good. Do not tempt me! I dare not take it, not even to keep it safe, unused."[6] As Bradley Birzer points out about the Ring's allure, "Other characters become tempted by it throughout the story: Galadriel, Boromir, and Denethor, to name just a few. The former resists, the latter two fail, and it proves their ultimate undoing."[7] Gandalf knows the Ring will attempt to twist one's greatest strength into one's greatest downfall. Pity is so central to Gandalf's identity that he realizes he must not allow his strength to be a vulnerability.

As the Istari arrive in Middle-earth to oppose Sauron, who seems to be rising again after the Ring was cut from his hand, one of their primary

---

[5] Tolkien, *The Silmarillion*, 16.

[6] Tolkien, *The Lord of the Rings*, 61.

[7] Bradley J. Birzer, *J. R. R. Tolkien's Sanctifying Myth: Understanding Middle-earth* (Wilmington, DE: Intercollegiate Studies Institute, 2009), chap. 5, Digital Edition.

responsibilities is "to move Elves and Men and all living things of good will to valiant deeds."[8] Gandalf does this powerfully by continually urging the White Council to assault Sauron in Dol Guldur and free Mirkwood of his oppressive presence. The White Council's confrontation did not ultimately defeat Sauron, who had already been preparing to withdraw to the land of Mordor. Despite motivating the powerful to valiant deeds, those valiant deeds do not start the chain of events that ultimately lead to Sauron's destruction. The final downfall of Sauron begins in earnest with the delivery of an unexpected invitation to an ordinary Hobbit.

Just before assaulting Dol Guldur, Gandalf knocks on a round, green door. "I am looking for someone to share in an adventure that I am arranging, and it's very difficult to find anyone."[9] Despite being "good-morninged by Belladonna Took's son, as if [he were] selling buttons at the door," he persistently pushes Bilbo to consider going on an adventure to the Lonely Mountain.[10] While Bilbo lists all the reasons that adventures are

---

[8] Tolkien, *The Silmarillion*, 309.

[9] J.R.R. Tolkien, *The Hobbit* (New York: Houghton Mifflin Harcourt, 1995), 4.

[10] Ibid., 5.

miserable, Gandalf persuades him to consider going because it will be "very good for you — and profitable too, very likely, if you ever get over it."[11] Gandalf implies that this adventure will result in more than just financial benefits. Although the story remained unfinished by J.R.R. Tolkien, in *The Quest for Erebor*, Gandalf appears to be concerned that as Bilbo grew older, "he was getting rather greedy and fat, and his old desires had dwindled down to a sort of private dream."[12] Someone in that condition would undoubtedly benefit from being given a slight push out of the door.

As the story progresses, Bilbo indeed does grow in a variety of ways. He burglarizes trolls, fights spiders, sneaks his companions out of Elvish prison, bravely ventures into Smaug's lair, and stands up to Thorin's belligerent resistance to sharing any of his treasure. He becomes stronger, cleverer, and wiser. Gandalf notices this near the end of the story, as they are returning to Bag End, and remarks, "Something is the matter with you! You are not the hobbit that you were."[13] Immediately before this statement,

---

[11] Tolkien, *The Hobbit*, 6.

[12] J.R.R. Tolkien, *Unfinished Tales of Numenor and Middle-earth*, ed. Christopher Tolkien (New York: Houghton Mifflin Harcourt, 1980), 308.

[13] Tolkien, *The Hobbit*, 302.

Bilbo is reciting a poem that begins, "Roads go ever ever on," a clear nod to the new spirit that has grown within him.[14] Rather than trying to avoid adventures altogether, he has learned that the road really does go on forever. While there is a comfort to returning home, as the verse concludes, that does not mean the adventure ends absolutely at its seeming completion. Stratford Caldecott summarizes, "Not only is Bilbo himself transformed by his adventures, but he also becomes a transformative influence on others, a catalyst for spiritual growth."[15] This adventure has more benefit than simply the small amount of treasure he brought home from the Lonely Mountain. Looking back on the events of Bilbo's inclusion in The Quest for Erebor, Gandalf concludes, "I knew in my heart that Bilbo must go with him, or the whole quest would be a failure — or, as I should say now, the far more important events by the way would not come to pass."[16] Gandalf's sentiment is a clear allusion to the finding of the Ring and its destruction that was brought nearer by Bilbo reaching around in the dark.

---

[14] Tolkien, *The Hobbit*, 302.

[15] Stratford Caldecott, *The Power of the Ring: The Spiritual Vision Behind the Lord of the Rings and The Hobbit* (New York: The Crossroad Publishing Company, 2012), chap. 2, Digital Edition.

[16] Tolkien, *Unfinished Tales of Numenor and Middle-earth*, 309.

Gandalf does not emphasize Bilbo's pity at the conclusion of *The Hobbit*, but he discusses that at length with Frodo at the beginning of *The Lord of the Rings*. Within the text of *The Hobbit* during the episode with Gollum under the Misty Mountains, little is said about Bilbo's pity. He begins to justify why it would be acceptable to kill Gollum, but ultimately "a sudden understanding, a pity mixed with horror, welled up in Bilbo's heart: a glimpse of endless unmarked days without light or hope of betterment, hard stone, cold fish, sneaking and whispering."[17] Despite Gollum's murderous intent, Bilbo could not bring himself to strike an unarmed opponent; he shows mercy. However, in *The Hobbit* itself, there is very little philosophical examination of this decision. When discussing the events with Frodo later, Gandalf explains, "It was Pity that stayed his hand. Pity, and Mercy: not to strike without need. And he has been well rewarded, Frodo. Be sure that he took so little hurt from the evil, and escaped in the end, because he began his ownership of the Ring so."[18] Had someone crueler discovered the Ring and the same scenario played out, Gollum may have been slain. Not only would this have interfered with

---

[17] Tolkien, *The Hobbit*, 87.

[18] Tolkien, *The Lord of the Rings*, 59.

the conclusion of *The Lord of the Rings*, but Bilbo would have become more like Gollum, a soul corrupted by the murderous acquisition of the Ring.

Gandalf does not conclude his remarks there, however. He prophesies that Bilbo's pity will also have some future effect, even if the exact details are uncertain. "I have not much hope that Gollum can be cured before he dies, but there is a chance of it. And he is bound up with the fate of the Ring. My heart tells me that he has some part to play yet, for good or ill, before the end; and when that comes, the pity of Bilbo may rule the fate of many -- yours not least."[19] Gandalf has been especially sensitive to and developed his sense of pity from his youth. If anyone were in a position to understand the power of pity and its connection to the "endurance of hope" as taught by Nienna, it would be Gandalf.[20]

Tolkien scholarship has long affirmed Gandalf's fulfillment of the Prophetic archetype. Gandalf has been identified as a partial Christ figure by many Tolkien scholars. Many seem to agree that, just as Jesus Christ held the three offices of the Priest, Prophet, and King, Tolkien used three characters, Frodo, Gandalf, and Aragorn, respectively, to

---

[19] Tolkien, *The Lord of the Rings*, 59.

[20] Tolkien, *The Silmarillion*, 16.

represent each of these three roles. Of Gandalf as Prophet, Birzer writes, "Like a true prophet, Gandalf, the servant of the Flame Imperishable, inspires men to use their gifts for the greater good of society, to live up to the best of the past, and to transmit this tradition to future generations."[21] Donald Williams concurs, "Gandalf is the Prophet. He is an unerring source of not just wisdom but also vision. He is the one who sees what needs to be done and can find people willing to do it. He gives people the faith to look beyond the needs of the moment to the needs of Middle-earth."[22] Peter Kreeft connects these three offices to the main powers of the soul: mind, emotions, and will. He connects Gandalf, the prophet, to the will, which connects directly to Gandalf's purpose to inspire the people of Middle-earth.[23]

When Gandalf is prophesying about Gollum's future role in the fate of the Ring, he has already inspired the White Council to act against Sauron, but he has also inspired an upper-middle-class

---

[21] Birzer, *J. R. R. Tolkien's Sanctifying Myth*, chap. 4.

[22] Donald Williams, *An Encouraging Thought: The Christian Worldview in the Writings of J. R. R. Tolkien* (Cambridge, OH: Christian Publishing House, 2018), chap. 1, Digital Edition.

[23] Peter Kreeft, *The Philosophy of Tolkien* (San Francisco: Ignatius Press, 2005), Conclusion, Digital Edition.

Hobbit to go on an adventure he does not want to go on. He did not just inspire anyone, though: he inspired Bilbo Baggins, a Hobbit whose disposition would be to show pity on a wretched, almost demonic creature that wants to kill him in a dark cave. All of this has elevated to a point where he can now inspire another Hobbit, encouraging him to pity Gollum.

Frodo's first encounter with Gollum demonstrates the power of Gandalf's inspiration. Sam immediately wants to kill Gollum, believing that he intends to kill them in their sleep. Frodo doubts this, and "It seemed to Frodo then that he heard, quite plainly but far off, voices out of the past: *What a pity Bilbo did not stab the vile creature, when he had a chance! Pity? It was Pity that stayed his hand. Pity, and Mercy: not to strike without need.*"[24] Reflecting on his recollection of Gandalf's words, Frodo states, "I will not touch the creature. For now that I see him, I do pity him."[25] At this moment, Frodo can kill Gollum. Just as Bilbo displayed pity by refusing to strike an unarmed victim, Frodo shows pity as well. The chief difference between Bilbo and Frodo is that Frodo began at a place of distrust and

[24] Tolkien, *The Lord of the Rings*, 615.

[25] Ibid.

dislike before being inspired by Gandalf months before to consider pity a viable option. Without that inspiration, this scenario could have played out entirely differently as well.

As the story comes to one of its most intense moments, Frodo decides not to destroy the Ring. He claims the Ring, puts it on, and succumbs to its power. Gollum bites the Ring off his finger before slipping into the fires of Mount Doom, destroying himself and it simultaneously. As Sam helps Frodo escape the mountain, Frodo notes, "But do you remember Gandalf's words: *Even Gollum may have something yet to do?* But for him, Sam, I could not have destroyed the Ring. The Quest would have been in vain, even at the bitter end. So let us forgive him! For the Quest is achieved, and now all is over."[26] In a letter to Amy Ronald, Tolkien commented on Frodo's failure by writing, "In this case the cause (not the 'hero') was triumphant, because by the exercise of pity, mercy, and forgiveness of injury, a situation was produced in which all was redressed and disaster averted. Gandalf certainly foresaw this."[27] Gandalf foresaw this event, so he stepped into his

[26] Tolkien, *The Lord of the Rings*, 947.

[27] J.R.R. Tolkien, *The Letters of J.R.R. Tolkien*, eds. Christopher Tolkien and Humphrey Carpenter (New York: HarperCollins, 2012), Letter 192, Digital Edition.

role as mentor to prepare Frodo for this moment. As Birzer recognizes, "Though Frodo failed in the end, overcome as he was by desire and greed, he succeeded at a much greater task: living out the advice of Gandalf and performing Christ-like acts of mercy to Gollum."[28] He served as more than just a prophet who foresaw the future; he served as a mentor who anticipated the future and prepared Frodo for his fate.

Although Gandalf's ordained mission was complete, as he told Aragorn when Sauron was defeated, the impact of his training can be seen even after the main quest has been completed. As the Hobbits return to a bleak and despairing Shire, Gandalf warns them that challenges are ahead. Merry optimistically points out that Gandalf is with them, so their mission might be somewhat easier. Gandalf responds, "I am not coming to the Shire. You must settle its affairs yourselves; that is what you have been trained for. Do you not yet understand? My time is over: it is no longer my task to set things to rights, nor to help folk to do so. And as for you, my dear friends, you will need no help. You are grown up now. Grown indeed very high; among the great you are, and I have no longer any fear at all for any

[28] Birzer, *J. R. R. Tolkien's Sanctifying Myth*, chap. 3.

of you."[29] Much like Bilbo, the four Hobbits have matured through the journey they have undertaken.

Gandalf even goes as far as to say that they have been trained to defend their homeland. If they had not gone on this adventure, they most likely would have fallen, just like many of their kinsmen, but because of the experience and instruction they have received, they are prepared to do what must be done on their own. As Caldecott writes, "The success of the hobbits in dealing with this final peril would not have been possible — would certainly not have been believable — if they had not experienced the epic adventure as a whole, and if we had not seen them transformed into heroes of song and legend; so that when they are plunged back into the banality of the Shire they are able to defeat the evil that they find with the grace — the gifts — that they have received in their travels."[30] Training typically implies a degree of intentionality, however. A trainer provides the instruction to the trainee. In this case, the quest functions as the trainer, and Gandalf provides the intentionality, as he was the one who put all four Hobbits on this mission. He presents the mission to Frodo at the beginning, even before Frodo

[29] Tolkien, *The Lord of the Rings*, 996.

[30] Caldecott, *The Power of the Ring*, chap. 3.

embraces it himself in Rivendell.[31] He pulls an eavesdropping Sam into the quest by his ear.[32] He advocates before Elrond to include Merry and Pippin in the Fellowship.[33] Gandalf's impact as the prophetic mentor extends beyond his active role in the plot. Because of the actions he took, they changed not only the present but also the future. He advocated for including the Hobbits on the quest, and as a result of that advocacy, they were able to defeat Saruman and free their homeland.

Gandalf's designated mission was to defeat Sauron. He performed many great feats of heroism on the battlefield and provided sage advice to the free people of Middle-earth. It may be easy to look towards these monumental tasks and conclude that these were the chief way in which Gandalf defeated Sauron. However, Sauron was not defeated in one moment. Sauron was defeated by serious conversations and momentary decisions of pity, inspired by Gandalf, the prophetic mentor.

This essay is dedicated to Holly Ordway, a prophetic mentor for many of us here at An Unexpected Journal.

---

[31] Tolkien, *The Lord of the Rings*, 61.

[32] Ibid., 63.

[33] Ibid., 276.

Middle-earth and the Middle Ages

Joseph Pearce on the Influence of Beowulf

Arguably the most important literary influence on *The Lord of the Rings*, the Anglo-Saxon epic, *Beowulf*, helps us understand the way in which Tolkien both conceals and reveals the deepest meaning in his own work.

Probably dating from the early eighth century, making it contemporaneous with the lives of Saints Boniface and Bede, *Beowulf* is a wonderful and wonder-filled narrative animated by the rich Christian spirit of the culture from which it sprang, brimming over with allegorical potency and evangelical zeal. It also conveys a deep awareness of classical antiquity, drawing deep inspirational draughts from Virgil's *Aeneid*, highlighting the Saxon poet's awareness of his place within an unbroken cultural continuum.

Tolkien translated *Beowulf* in its entirety, though his translation would not finally be published until 2014, and he wrote a scholarly essay on the epic, "The Monsters and the Critics", which is considered by many to be the most masterful critique of the poem ever written. Clearly Tolkien knew *Beowulf* well, perhaps better than anyone else of his generation, and there is no denying its seminal and definitive influence on his own work. Most obvious are the inescapable parallels between the dragon episode in *Beowulf* and the similar episode in *The Hobbit*. It is, however, in a more subtle way that the Anglo-Saxon epic can be seen to have left its inspirational fingerprints on *The Lord of the Rings*.

Beowulf is divided into three sections in which the eponymous hero fights three different monsters. In the first two episodes, as Beowulf confronts and ultimately defeats Grendel and then Grendel's mother, the work is primarily a narrative in which the theological dimension is subsumed parabolically, especially in the recurring motif that human will and strength is insufficient, in the absence of divine assistance, to defeat the power of evil. This is presumably an orthodox riposte to the heresy of Pelagianism, which plagued Saxon England and which is a major preoccupation of Bede in his *Ecclesiastical History*, probably written at around the same time as *Beowulf*.[1] [2] *The Lord of the Rings* adopts a very similar approach in the way that it subsumes the presence of grace within the fabric of the story, unobtrusively and yet inescapably, something which is beyond the scope of our present discussion. It is, however, the allegorical technique that the *Beowulf* poet employs in the final section of the epic which most illumines the technique that Tolkien will himself employ in his own epic, emulating the anonymous poet who had taught him more than anyone else about the art of storytelling.

The dragon section of *Beowulf* commences with the theft of "a gem-studded goblet" from the dragon's hoard, an act which gained the thief nothing but which provoked the destructive wrath of the dragon.[3] Beowulf takes eleven comrades with him as he goes to meet the dragon in combat, plus the thief, "the one who had started all this strife" and

---

[1] The Pelagians believed that men could forge their own eternal destiny, earning themselves a place in heaven by obeying the teachings of Christ through a triumph of the human will over temptation. Such a belief denied the need for grace and therefore denied the need for the Church and her sacraments.

[2] There is much disagreement about the exact dating of *Beowulf*, its composition being shrouded in mystery. The present author agrees with those, including Tolkien, who believe it was written sometime between the mid-seventh and mid-eighth century.

[3] All quotes from *Beowulf* are from Seamus Heaney's translation (New York: W. W. Norton & Company, 2002).

who "was now added as a thirteenth to their number". Unlike the eleven who had accompanied their lord willingly, the thief was "press-ganged and compelled" to go with them, acting as their unwilling guide to the dragon's den. Clearly the *Beowulf* poet is employing numerical signification to draw parallels between Beowulf's fight to the death with the dragon (an iconic signification of the Devil) and Christ's own fight to the death with the power of evil in His Passion. Equally clearly, *Beowulf* is not a formal or crude allegory because no character in the epic is merely a personified abstraction. Beowulf is not literally Christ, though he could be called a figure of Christ, one who is meant to remind us of Christ; the dragon is not literally Satan, though he or it is clearly intended to remind us of the Devil himself. Similarly, the thief is not Judas (nor Adam) but is intended to remind us of the disciple whose act of treachery brought about his lord's death, and the other eleven are of course reminiscent of the other eleven apostles. The numerical coincidence exhibits the poet's intention of drawing analogous connections to the Gospel narrative of the Passion without ever succumbing to the level of formal or crude allegory. Beowulf is always Beowulf, even though he is meant to remind us of Christ.

Continuing the allusive parallels, this time with Christ's agony in the Garden, we are told that, on the eve of battle, Beowulf is "sad at heart, unsettled yet ready, sensing his death." Later, as battle is about to commence, Beowulf's appointed followers, "that hand-picked troop." "broke ranks and ran for their lives." all except one, Wiglaf, who emerges as the signifier of St. John, the only one of Christ's apostles who remained at his side during the Crucifixion. Wiglaf reprimands his comrades for their cowardice in deserting their lord, reminding them that Beowulf had "picked us out from the army deliberately, honored us and judged us fit for this action".

Prior to his death, Beowulf instructs Wiglaf to order his men to build a burial mound in remembrance of him. After his death, ten shamefaced warriors emerge from the woods, indicating that the thief was not among them. At the epic's conclusion there are once again twelve warriors riding ceremoniously around the burial mound, which had been duly constructed in accordance with Beowulf's command, indicating that the traitor had been replaced by a new member, reminiscent of the appointment of St. Matthias to replace Judas as the twelfth apostle. Although nobody would suggest that *Beowulf* is an allegory in the formal sense, its being bereft of the personified abstractions that are the mark of formal allegory, it is clear that the poet intends his audience to see suggestive parallels between Beowulf's sacrifice of himself in the battle against evil and that of the archetypal sacrifice of God Himself on Calvary. For the Christian, and the *Beowulf* poet was indubitably Christian, all acts of genuine love involve the laying down of our lives for another. Furthermore, all those who genuinely love in this way are ipso facto figures of Christ, from whom all genuine love flows and towards whom all genuine love points. In true life as in true literature all those who live and love like Christ are Christ-like and, as such, can be said to be figures of Christ. Christ is the *archetype* of which all virtuous men, in fact and in fiction, are *types*. The *Beowulf* poet shows this through the use of numerical clues. Tolkien does something very similar in his own work, emulating the work of his Anglo-Saxon mentor.

Tolkien signifies the deepest meaning of *The Lord of the Rings* in the clue he supplies with regard to the specific date of the destruction of the Ring. The Ring is destroyed on March 25, the most significant and important date on the Christian calendar. This is the feast of the Annunciation, the date on which the Word is made flesh, when God becomes man. It is also, according to tradition, the historic date of the Crucifixion, a fact which is all too often forgotten by modern Christians because Good Friday is celebrated as a moveable feast which falls on a different date each year. This is what the *Catholic Encyclopedia* says about the significance of March 25:

> All Christian antiquity . . . recognized the 25th of March as the actual day of Our Lord's death. The opinion that the Incarnation also took place on that date is found in the pseudo-Cyprianic work *De Pascha Computus*, c. 240. It argues that the coming of Our Lord and His death must have coincided with the creation and fall of Adam. And since the world was created in spring, the Saviour was also conceived and died shortly after the equinox of spring. Similar fanciful calculations are found in the early and later Middle Ages . . . Consequently the ancient martyrologies assign to the 25th of March the creation of Adam and the crucifixion of Our Lord; also, the fall of Lucifer, the passing of Israel through the Red Sea and the immolation of Isaac.[4]

[4] Frederick Holweck, "The Feast of the Annunciation." *The Catholic Encyclopedia.* Vol. 1. (New York: Robert Appleton Company,

Let's recall at this juncture that Tolkien is both a Catholic and a very scholarly mediaevalist. He would have known of the symbolic significance of this date and his ascribing of this particular date as that on which the Ring is destroyed has palpable and indeed seismic consequences with regard to the deepest moral and theological meaning of *The Lord of the Rings*.

A great mediaeval work of literature that employs the same allegorical use of significant dates that Tolkien employs to convey deep moral and theological meaning is Chaucer's "Nun's Priest's Tale". In this parable about the Fall of Man and his subsequent redemption by Christ on the Cross (masquerading as a fable about a rooster), we are told that the story takes place thirty-two days after the beginning of March, "the month in which the world began . . . when God first made man."[5] Apart from Chaucer's reference to the theological significance of March, he signals that Chauntecleer's "Fall" (Adam's) and the Fox's (Satan's) happens on April 1, i.e. April Fool's Day!

1907), accessed October 16, 2021, http://www.newadvent.org/cathen/01542a.htm.

[5] For the sake of clarity, Chaucer's original English has been modified. The purist, I hope, will forgive me.

In following his mediaeval mentors in their employment and deployment of allegorical clues to deepen the theological dimension of their stories, Tolkien was infusing the genius of Christendom and its literary giants into his own timeless epic. In doing so, he was thereby situating his own work firmly within that tradition. He was also deploying those same clues to signify that *The Lord of the Rings* was working its magic most profoundly on the level of theology. Since Original Sin and the One Ring are both destroyed on the same theologically-charged date, they become inextricably interwoven so that the Ring is synonymous with Sin itself. With his Ring, Tolkien weds his own work morally and theologically to the deepest truths of Christianity, forging it in the flames of his lifelong faith.

Contrary Winds: Tolkien's Priority of Faith and Family as Presented in Tolkien's Modern Reading

Donald W. Catchings, Jr. on
Tolkien's Personal Values

It is difficult to be immersed in a world of contrary winds and hold steady to one's course. And yet, this is precisely what J.R.R. Tolkien did. Although he is remembered primarily as the author of *The Lord of the Rings, The Hobbit,* and his larger Legendarium and secondarily as an academic, when one is willing to look at his work in-depth and, even just slightly, past his work as an author and academic, they will find what truly defined the man. As is presented in complement to Holly Ordway's thesis in her most recent work published through Word on Fire Academic, *Tolkien's Modern Reading:*

Middle-earth Beyond the Middle Ages, Tolkien was one of those rare men who dedicated himself primarily to faith and family. What makes him exceptional is that such a prioritization is very rarely practiced in reality. An examination of his life beyond the Legendarium, which is necessary to fully understand his Legendarium, presents Tolkien as an example of more than a man of impeccable scholarship or a Christian who produced good apologetic work. Within her well-researched exposition concerning the modern world's influence in Tolkien's life, Ordway reveals how Tolkien exemplifies what it means to be a faithful Christian and father who does not allow the world to redefine him. Rather, through faithful perseverance, Tolkien stays the course set by God and tradition.

Since the Enlightenment, a focal point of the academy has been to remake the world in the image of man's reason and to cast aside the "fine-fabling" of tradition which employs the imagination to experience "a sacramental view of reality," to experience God.[1] In this setting, it has become increasingly difficult to balance one's Christian faith and scholarship. This has not occurred because the

[1] Holly Ordway, *Tolkien's Modern Reading: Middle-earth Beyond the Middle Ages* (Park Ridge: Word on Fire Academic, 2021), 256.

Christian faith and intelligence are at odds, but because the worldview of the Christian faith has become, in the wake of Enlightenment thought, unpopular and mischaracterized as a backward looking hindrance, especially to an educated person.[2] His place in the changing of times did not escape Tolkien. He read works of skeptics and anti-Christian figures like H.G. Wells — whose science fiction he held "in high regard;" also, he was no stranger to works of James Joyce — *Anna Livia Plurabelle* (known in its final form as *Finnegans Wake*) was a possible influence on Tolkien's "Errantry" — or Sinclair Lewis — *Babbitt* was named by Tolkien as a source for the name, hobbit.[3] The works of these individuals provided critiques which have caused, for some, or echoed, for others, a disenchantment with traditional faith (not just Christian) that marked Tolkien's generation; therefore, the unexpectedness of their influence

---

[2] Directly attacking Christianity, Neitzche says, "One concept removed, a single reality substituted in its place — and the whole of Christianity crumbles to nothing!" Friedrich Neitzsche, *Twilight of the Idols and the Anti-Christ* (London: Penguin Classics, 2003), 164.

In a snide remark against religion as a whole, Hitchens claims that "religion was the race's first (and worst) attempt to make sense of reality." Christopher Hitchens, *The Portable Atheist: Essential Reading for the Nonbeliever* (Philadelphia: Da Capo Press, 2007), loc. 244, Kindle.

[3] Ordway, *Tolkien's Modern Reading*, 232, 246, 288, and 296-297.

should not be considered of small account. Tolkien was intellectually immersed in the modern world, "engaging" it through his fantasy work, without taking on its negative thinking.[4] Thus, the fact that a first-rate and modern scholar such as Tolkien never wavered in his Christian faith is a testament of his vigor and an important model for Christians in the modern world, and even more so for up-and-coming Christian scholars. However, there is another element that made Tolkien's faithfulness to his religion even more difficult; he was not just a Christian but a Catholic, and a convert to Catholicism at that.

It was only within the century that Tolkien was born (1892) that Catholics had been accepted back into Parliament (1829), and only about two decades before his birth (1871) were Catholics permitted back into British universities like Tolkien's alma mater, Oxford. Therefore, it should be easy to understand that Tolkien's chosen branch of orthodox Christianity, Catholicism, placed him into a sort of double-minority position in the academic world. And yet, as Ordway uncovers chapter by chapter in *Tolkien's Modern Reading*, it is "a manifestation of his Catholic faith" that supplied

[4] Ordway, *Tolkien's Modern Reading*, 338-339.

Tolkien with the "extensive, expansive, inclusive" taste which laid the foundation for his scholarship and Legendarium.[5]

As stated above, Ordway's research shows that Tolkien read Wells, Joyce, and S. Lewis, which, when considering the variance of their fictional genres, proves an interest ranging from science fiction to cultural satire. But Tolkien had a taste for literature that spread far beyond such "adult" genres. Beatrix Potter held "an important place on the bookshelves of Tolkien's children," but that is because Tolkien was, himself, a fan of tales like *Peter Rabbit*, specifically the way the tales are rhythmically laid out.[6] Tolkien once suggested that a Tom Bombadil book be made to physically mimic *Peter Rabbit*.[7] Tolkien was also a fan of fairy-tales such as Andrew Lang's *Fairy Books*; in 1939, Tolkien gave his lecture "On Fairy-stories" on the occasion of the University of St. Andrews annual lecture in commemoration of Andrew Lang, which was further developed into the critical essay of the same title.[8] Furthermore, though Tolkien read lasting names like George

---

[5] Ordway, *Tolkien's Modern Reading*, 273.

[6] Ibid., 92-93.

[7] Ibid.

[8] Ibid., 64.

MacDonald and Lewis Carroll, he was also influenced by authors whose works have not stood the test of time. For example, George Dasent's "Soria Moria Castle" had a role in Tolkien's invention of "Khazad-dum."[9] This wide-ranging taste in reading (along with the works unmentioned in-between), which also interspersed itself into Tolkien's writing, is very catholic indeed.

This is important because, Ordway consistently shows, Tolkien's Catholic faith and catholic proclivities did not act as a hindrance to his scholarship or imagination but as the very impetus of both.[10] Tolkien was a young convert to his, otherwise, lifelong religious traditions, traditions that had only recently been granted a parcel of the respect they are due (thus, prejudices naturally lingered).[11] Nonetheless, considering Tolkien's statement that "*The Lord of the Rings* is of course a

---

[9] Ordway, *Tolkien's Modern Reading*, 66.

[10] There is a difference in the term Catholic, with a capital C, and catholic with a lowercase c. The first is referring to the Catholic Church in Rome. The second is an adjective that means comprehensive or universal.

[11] For the reader to understand this historical claim, it should be noted that Tolkien began studying at Oxford in 1911, only sixty years after "the Catholic hierarchy had been restored to England and Wales" (Ordway, *Tolkien's Modern Reading*, 44) and forty years after Catholics had been allowed to become students at Oxford through the 1871 Universities Tests Act.

fundamentally religious and Catholic work," and, as Ordway argues, his "catholic taste in literature is . . . but a manifestation of his Catholic faith: extensive, expansive, inclusive," it seems safe to say that if not for his faithfulness to his Catholic traditions (his catholic taste), Tolkien would have produced a very different Legendarium.[12] This fact should encourage aspiring Christian apologists and academics alike to hold fast to the foundation of their religious traditions, while not utterly rejecting the modern world, even if their traditions are the minority position, for such a foundation is tried, true, and provides an objective guide to extensive, expansive, and inclusive scholarship.

One of the more interesting complements to Ordway's thesis is that Tolkien's faith not only guided him to be the remarkable man he was in the university, it also provided the grounds for an exceptional home life. Traditionally, Christianity places a great and blessed burden on the shoulders of Christian fathers — taking care of one's family is top priority. In 1 Corinthians 7, Ephesians 6, and Colossians 3, the Apostle Paul gives various

[12] J.R.R. Tolkien, "142 To Robert Murray, S.J." in *The Letters of J.R.R. Tolkien*, ed. by Humphrey Carpenter and Christopher Tolkien (Boston: Houghton Mifflin Harcourt, 2013), 172; Ordway, *Tolkien's Modern Reading*, 316.

statements that have guided Christians to understand the value and place of marriage and single life as it relates to ministry. Those who do not get married have more time to dedicate to God. This precept definitely plays out in the Catholic tradition, for those who are to be utterly dedicated to ministry, priests and nuns, are not permitted to be married. This prohibition is not in place because marriage and children are bad things or even a hindrance to one's faith. Instead, this prohibition is in place because it is recognized that if one gets married and has offspring, their primary responsibility is bringing their children up in faith and tradition; thus, they will not have as much time to dedicate to ministry outside of the home. Tolkien was a married man and father; for that reason, he was called by his faith to place his family above his own wants and desires, and to "raise them up in the discipline and instruction of the Lord."[13] This precept, of course, does not stop with one's call to minister to the world at large. This precept of priority is also applied to one's vocation. Such an attitude toward family priority can be clearly seen in Tolkien's home life.

C.S. Lewis once made a fitting evaluation when he said that Tolkien was the most married man he

---

[13] Eph 6:4, NET.

knew.[14] Unlike the nearly perpetual bachelor, Lewis, Tolkien married young. He was married for over five decades and had four children. His children, as well as grandchildren and great-grandchildren, were precious to him. As Ordway points out, "Tolkien made a point of spending time with his wife, daughter, and granddaughters as well as with his brother, sons, and grandsons" — along with more extended family members and even, to insert a more modern phrase, friends so close one might consider them adopted into the family.[15] One of his sons even claimed that Tolkien "possessed the ability . . . of combining fatherhood and friendship."[16] A striking fact that may speak to Tolkien's prioritization of family before work is that even much of his well-known work "had its origins in the context of Tolkien's family."[17] Included in this list would be *The Hobbit* and Tom Bombadil.

Tolkien's imaginative endeavors were trialed in his family storytelling and his lasting legacy is in large part due to his son, Christopher Tolkien. His family appears to have acted as more than a

---

[14] Ordway, *Tolkien's Modern Reading*, 32.

[15] Ibid.

[16] Ibid., 63.

[17] Ibid.

motivation to go to work and provide; they were an integral part of the development of his most lasting work — his Legendarium, and other fun imaginative works like *Father Christmas*.[18] By living out this precept, Tolkien provides another clear and remarkable example of the benefits and blessings that accompany following and integrating one's faith and traditions into the bedrock of their life.

Another point that makes this remarkable is the fact that prioritizing family and faith in a society that is ever-shifting away from work as a means to live to work as life itself is and staying true to Christianity in a culture that is evolving from a foundationally Christian to a post-Christian culture was certainly a minority position. And even more remarkable may be the fact that, in order to live out both minority positions, he did not cut himself or his family off from the world. While already a young family man, he was a soldier in the trenches of World War I. As a lifetime career, he was a professor at Oxford — one of the world's foremost universities. All four of his children even went on to

[18] For the reader who is not familiar with the backstory of Tolkien's *Father Christmas*, the work is a compilation of Tolkien's letters to his children. During the Christmas season, Tolkien would pen letters pretending to be Father Christmas, complete with original artwork and hand drawn postage stamps.

earn degrees at Oxford.[19] As is thoroughly uncovered by the scholarly research presented in *Tolkien's Modern Reading*, he was very widely read in modern literature — everything from Victorian children's literature to modern American science fiction were willingly and, often, enjoyably consumed by Tolkien. He was also ahead of the game in his use of recording devices and typewriters (a surprisingly modern man on this account). All in all, Tolkien was a very up-to-date man.

Staying up-to-date in a culture as blatantly contrary as Tolkien's without succumbing to the culture was a test. The moral fiber which had been foundational to his culture was breaking down and trying to reinvent itself. He, on the other hand, was doing his utmost to hold onto those moral values of faith and tradition that are tried, true, objective, and biblical. Tolkien passed this test; but not because he utterly shunned the contrary culture that surrounded him. Unlike what many have supposed to be true due to the official status given to Humphrey Carpenter's *J.R.R. Tolkien: A Biography*, the modern, contemporary, everyday world was not some dangerous business waiting outside Tolkien's front door but a welcomed part of his life. And, as

[19] Ordway, *Tolkien's Modern Reading*, 64.

Ordway notes, such a reality should be expected: "He was, after all, a man of letters, an academic in the field of English literature; he would have felt something approaching a professional responsibility to know what was being written in his day . . . quite apart from the fact that he was naturally a man with an abiding curiosity and interest in the world around him."[20]

Even outside of his literary career, Tolkien was a man who did not shy away from current issues: he read the newspaper daily; as a matter of fact, he was subscribed to three.[21] A more outstanding instance is the comment Tolkien made publicly in 1959 regarding Apartheid: "I have the hatred of apartheid in my bones."[22] This was not as hot of an issue at the time as the common person might assume for this statement preceded the massacre committed the next year which caused wide public outrage.[23] Still,

[20] Ordway, *Tolkien's Modern Reading*, 248.

[21] Ibid., 31.

[22] Ibid., 158. The reader may be interested to know that one reason Tolkien may have been so forthright about this issue, and why it seems to be near and dear to him, is because he was actually born in South Africa and his whole family were quite close to their indigenous African servants. If one is diligent enough in their research, it is even possible to find that there is a Tolkien family picture which includes said servants.

[23] Ibid.

Tolkien made his position known. And this is exactly what should be expected because Tolkien was not just a man of letters but a man of the Christian faith: a faith that is responsible for the foundation of human rights, rights which are rooted in the biblical claim of humanity's inherent value, *the imago dei*. He would have, as should the contemporary burgeoning and situated Christian scholar, felt something of a responsibility to speak plainly on such an affront to human rights. Moreover, having recently seen the atrocities of Germany in WWII, Tolkien would not have wanted a repeat of the horrendous acts perpetrated by "that ruddy little ignoramus" Hitler against the Jews.[24] Likewise, the contemporary Christian scholar should hate the evil of devaluing humanity and the price Christ paid for humanity via the restriction and stripping of human rights in their own time. Also, the Christian should not be afraid to speak plainly on behalf of the rights of their fellow human being, or voice their opinion about affronts to humanity.

As stated above, that Tolkien was a man so welcoming of the wider, modern world, is often a

---

[24] J.R.R. Tolkien, "45 To Michael Tolkien" in *The Letters of J.R.R. Tolkien*, ed. by Humphrey Carpenter and Christopher Tolkien (Boston: Houghton Mifflin Harcourt, 2013), 55.

surprise. That he allowed the modern world to influence him without altering who he was fundamentally, is also a surprise to many. More than this, that the modern world was impactful in the shaping of his Legendarium is unexpected.[25] However, though his "abiding, global popularity seems to require explanation," the explanation is not one that will come from a revelation of conformity. He was certainly not "an author who deliberately isolated himself from the modern world."[26] But he was also not an author who let the world change the views that he held dear. Tolkien's way of handling the world was what many might perceive as an oxymoron: he was a modern, up-to-date, forward thinking man who was firmly faithful to an ancient religion and a traditional way of thinking and seeing the world.

Tolkien was not some sort of backwards thinking Catholic who rejected the modern world for the sake of the medieval and, thus, took refuge in a hole in the ground so as to shield himself from the

---

[25] Ordway provides numerous examples of the modern world's influence on key elements in Tolkien's most famous works that are not just philological. One of the more fascinating examples is that the term Hobbit, as well as the accompanying characteristics and lifestyle, are influenced by Sinclair Lewis's George F. Babbitt (Ordway, *Tolkien's Modern Reading*, 288-289).

[26] Ordway, *Tolkien's Modern Reading*, 158.

contrary winds of such a stance. He was a critical thinker who weighed and measured the literature and current world around him with "critical faculties in gear."[27] From the perspective of a cautious character, Tolkien interpreted "the medieval world for his modern readers."[28] He was able to do this because he knew "both cultures, the old and the new" well enough to be able to grant "his insights."[29] Even if he did reject something, he did not reject it as utterly inconsequential; even if he rejected it, he did not, as is too common a trend currently, cancel it.

As is shown in *Tolkien's Modern Reading*, there was plenty of culture and literature that Tolkien did not agree with and still it influenced him, for "to reject something is to be influenced by it."[30] As an example, one may consider how Tolkien and Joyce both experimented with and enjoyed the sound of language — Ordway's discourse on the connection between *Anna Livia Plurabelle* and Tolkien's "Errantry" is an interesting addition to this topic — though Tolkien's purpose was more developed than

---

[27] Ordway, *Tolkien's Modern Reading*, 9.

[28] Ibid., 20.

[29] Ibid.

[30] Ibid., 24.

Joyce's.[31] Moreover, Tolkien and Joyce were contemporaries who reimagined myth in modern ways, though Joyce's "irreverence toward Homer's Odyssey" would not have set right with Tolkien.[32] Another example is that though H.G. Wells was unabashed in his "materialist, secularist view of history," Tolkien is not hesitant to consider Wells an Old Master of science fiction.[33] Also, the colonialist and racist perspectives presented in the children's stories of Alexander Macdonald and Herbert Haynes, stories that Tolkien admired, are certainly opposite the opinion's Tolkien expressed on such topics.[34] Tolkien did not agree with these artists on very important issues; yet they influenced his work. And considering the last example concerning racism, it may have been at the point of disagreement that these works most readily influenced Tolkien.

Rejection is not the same as cancellation, at least it is not in Tolkien's case, for rejection is, at times, only based on personal taste and not an objective standard. In regards to this point, it should be noted

---

[31] Ordway, *Tolkien's Modern Reading*, 297-298.

[32] Ibid., 297 and 338.

[33] Ibid., 231-232.

[34] Ibid., 169.

that Tolkien was an honest academic and Catholic that spoke his mind and criticized when needed. Tolkien's often overstated criticism of the draft for C.S. Lewis' *The Lion, the Witch and the Wardrobe*, is a good example of Tolkien's criticism without cancellation considering that, though he originally rejected it, he later suggested it to his granddaughter.[35]

Although only complementary to her thesis in *Tolkien's Modern Reading*, Ordway pronounces that Tolkien did not allow his faith and his work to work against each other. He did not allow his faith and his family to work against each other. He did not allow his work and his family to work against each other. He did not allow personal taste to deter his acknowledgment of a work's merit. He did not allow his immersion in the modern world to work against his traditional faith, and vice-versa. As a good Catholic, Tolkien properly prioritized and balanced faith, family, work, duty, and most every aspect of his life by adhering to the precepts of his Catholic faith. To say it more forthrightly than it may come across on the first reading of Ordway's work, Tolkien was certainly a man in the world but not of it.

---

[35] Ordway, *Tolkien's Modern Reading*, 109.

Thus, the modern Christian scholar should not fear or shun the modern world; they should not lock it outside their front door in fear that it might be some unappeased Angel of Death coming for their faith and tradition. Rather, the Christian scholar should take Tolkien's handling of a contrary world as a guide. The Christian scholar should welcome the outside world in with caution and with every intent to criticize it with honest integrity; to baptize it with a biblical worldview; to provide it with a different direction and not allow it to change one's own direction; and, albeit surprising to some, let the modern world be a positive influence that helps the Christian scholar's eyes open to their own blind spots and prejudices. The Christian scholar must play an integral role in the world but still stand out from it by holding steady, via faith and tradition, against the world's contrary winds.

Ordway's Myth-Busting Research: Tolkien's Modern Reading (A Review)

Ryan Grube on a Paradigm Shift

In her monumental study, *Tolkien's Modern Reading: Middle-earth Beyond the Middle Ages* (TMR), Holly Ordway debunks the popular misconception that J.R.R. Tolkien was an anti-modern medievalist whose inspiration came from the Middle Ages and who avoided influences more recent than *Beowulf*. This error, planted by "rogue" biographers such as William Ready, Daniel Grota, and especially Humphrey Carpenter, has been at the root of what Ordway deems a "critical imbalance" in Tolkien scholarship, and correcting it is the first major accomplishment of her book.[1] This she achieves by

[1] Holly Ordway, *Tolkien's Modern Reading: Middle-Earth Beyond the Middle Ages* (Park Ridge, IL: Word on Fire, 2021), 276-279. Notwithstanding Carpenter's official status as the only authorized

mustering evidence that Tolkien read and incorporated elements from works of more recent, particularly "modern" vintage. Ordway writes:

> Where, then, do we turn for evidence of Tolkien's modern reading? It comes from a range of sources: Tolkien's own writings, published and unpublished; interviews with him; accounts by family, friends, colleagues, and students; biographical studies; and finally, material in Christina Scull and Wayne G. Hammond's magisterial *J.R.R. Tolkien Companion and Guide*.[2]

In the course of presenting these materials, Ordway evaluates their impact on the works related to *The Lord of The Rings* known collectively as the Legendarium.[3] Her investigation of these data demonstrates both an impressive depth of research and a compelling engagement with Tolkien's own imaginative source material, and it compares favorably to other recent studies, such as Oronzo

---

biographer of Tolkien, Ordway's meticulous study proves that in his case the "rogue" epithet is quite well deserved.

[2] Ordway, *Tolkien's Modern Reading,* 30.

[3] e.g. *The Silmarillion, Beren and Lúthien, The Adventures of Tom Bombadil,* etc.

Cilli's *Tolkien's Library: An Annotated Checklist.*[4] Cilli's *Library* was published two years prior to *TMR*; it is methodologically sound and presents an impressively comprehensive list; yet it is valuable primarily to researchers, as it is quite literally an annotated bibliography. *TMR*, on the other hand, is not simply a list of modern books owned by Tolkien, but a work of literary criticism which discusses the author's assimilation and creative adaptation of these materials. Ordway's purpose is therefore more involved:

> it is not enough simply to identify a source or influence and stop there in foolish triumph. We must go further and be attentive to context, purpose, style, effect, and, above all, meaning; we must ask 'How does Tolkien use it? What insight do we gain from having discerned this connection? What does this tell us about his writings and even about him and his own creative processes?[5]

Limiting herself to English language "works of fiction, poetry, and drama published after 1850 . . . that we know for certain Tolkien read, she

[4] Oronzo Cilli, *Tolkien's Library: An Annotated Checklist* (Edinburgh: Luna Press Publishing, 2019).

[5] Ordway, *Tolkien's Modern Reading,* 41.

concentrates on how such works might have played a role in the development of Tolkien's Legendarium, adopting the distinction made by C.S. Lewis between "sources" and "influences" as useful terms to guide the investigation.[6] According to this understanding, a source is a work that contributes "content or substance, be it a character, a plot, a theme, an image," while an influence involves "manner or form, the style in which an author approaches his work or the shape he gives it."[7] Ordway identifies one more process by which Tolkien's modern reading can be connected to his writing, labeling it "influence-by-opposition." As opposed to source and influence (matters of content and form, respectively), influence-by-opposition occurs by way of bad example, for instance something Tolkien read that he wished to avoid emulating, or which provoked him to improve upon when he tried it himself in his own writing.

Under these rubrics, Ordway exhibits skillful detective work in ferreting out likely origins for specific events, place names, dramatic technique, tone, atmosphere, etc., yet she is careful to avoid reducing her study to mere textual archaeology. She

[6] Ordway, *Tolkien's Modern Reading,* 27.

[7] Ibid., 33-34.

explains that "we aim rather continually to be moving both back and forth -- now backward to what Tolkien read, now forward to the effects that his reading may have had," and her concern is discerning these effects not only on Tolkien's Legendarium, but also upon "our own understanding of the man and the workings of his imagination."[8]

Given the amount of material she distills into three hundred pages, it is impressive how much Ordway accomplishes in so limited a space. Compositionally, *TMR* is divided into twelve chapters: the first two set the stage for and delimit the scope of Ordway's project; the final gives a summary and concluding remarks; and the intervening chapters provide accumulated data and commentary. These middle chapters, which comprise the bulk of *TMR*, proceed roughly along chronological lines. Chapters three and four begin with an inspection of Victorian and then "Post-Victorian" children's literature, respectively. Next, the works of George MacDonald are treated in chapter five before discussion turns to the thriller-adventure genre stories of S.R. Crockett, Alexander MacDonald, Herbert Hayens, John Buchan, and J.M.

[8] Ordway, *Tolkien's Modern Reading,* 39.

Barrie, which comprise chapter six, "Boy's Own Adventure." After these, William Morris and Rider Haggard each receive full chapters of their own. Then the examination reverts to a more genre based approach centered around science fiction, "fine fabling," and an assortment of authors Ordway collects under the term "Catholic."[9] [10]

Since she attends to these works only insofar as they relate to Tolkien's Legendarium or his creative process, not all books and authors wind up with an equal amount of discussion.[11] The *dispositio* thus initially produces a slight sense of lopsidedness or asymmetry. However, this is a very minor quibble, and indeed the impression does not last long, especially after one considers Tolkien did not arrange his personal reading for the convenience of literary critics and historians! Not everything

---

[9] Ordway, *Tolkien's Modern Reading,* 225. "stories that present the marvelous, the uncanny, the preternatural; high romance and Gothic tales; literature that embraces the mystical and numinous, that finds room for a sacramental view of reality. Here we find writers who, in many cases, do not fit comfortably into other categories, or who no longer suit our modern tastes as readers -- but who were important to their original readers."

[10] Ibid., 248. This enables Ordway to discuss specifically *Roman Catholic* literary figures, but she also means 'catholic' in its broad and inclusive sense, and uses it to round up "everybody" not yet mentioned.

[11] Most of these middle chapters come in under twenty pages, chapter 6 being the exception at 57 pages.

Tolkien read equally influenced his Legendarium. Not every author had the same type or degree of impact. Therefore the range of Ordway's commentary will necessarily follow suit: sometimes drilling down into minutiae, other times zooming out for more generalized observations, but always borne of a thorough analysis of the connections between Tolkien's creative inputs and his own creative output. From this point of view, Ordway has actually done her readers a service. Rather than impose some uniform interpretive grid to effect a false sense of evenness or proportionality, her approach leads us on a tour that wends and wanders across 200 titles from 148 authors, and does so in a sensical, compelling fashion.[12] The prose is lucid, the arguments cogent. Her familiarity with the Legendarium and careful inspection of source texts is compendious, and the work brims with wit and personality throughout.[13]

As a work of literary criticism, *TMR* bears not a few resemblances to Michael Ward's 2008 *Planet*

---

[12] Ordway, *Tolkien's Modern Reading,* 275; 295.

[13] Ibid., 14. See for example the clever headline "The mythical Tollewis"; also the footnote on p. 289 regarding Stephen Colbert and Chance the Rapper.

Narnia.[14] Both projects dispel misconceptions about an Inkling, particularly ones concerning inspirational input and compositional choices. Both retrieve an old-school literary criticism, less intent on imposing politically charged 'critical lenses' and more interested in exploring questions of literary-historical value. Both Ward and Ordway deepen our appreciation of the fantasy worlds created by Lewis and Tolkien by their study of the material and formal causes at work in the creative processes of the two Inklings. Ward points us skyward and shows the link between the seven *Chronicles of Narnia* and the pre-Copernican cosmology of the seven heavens.[15] Ordway uses the earth to illustrate the simple but oft-ignored fact that a fertile imagination such as Tolkien's requires . . . well, *fertilizer.* "Many and varied leaves from the woods and forests of British and American literature," she writes, became the "leaf-mould" and then the mulch which nourished Tolkien's creativity and "provided him with the nutrients that he could draw up into

---

[14] Michael Ward, *Planet Narnia: The Seven Heavens in The Imagination of C.S. Lewis* (Oxford: Oxford UP, 2008).

[15] Ibid., 223; 234-239. Lewis employed planetary imagery in fashioning a literary atmosphere which conveys an imaginative experience of the medieval worldview, thereby exposing the reader to important facets of the Divine nature.

new stories."[16] Her research is tightly focused on "the more modern trees that we know [Tolkien] to have surveyed," and it is on account of this specificity that Ordway succeeds in establishing a new paradigm in Tolkien studies.[17]

To be sure, this paradigm shift has been a long time in coming. Comparisons between Tolkien and some of his modernist contemporaries were not unprecedented in the years before the "rogue biographers" myth took root but have only gradually gained traction since. Ordway notes that already in 1974, Colin Wilson had compared Tolkien's *Lord of the Rings* with Proust and T.S. Eliot, and "on the basis of Tolkien's writings alone, placed him firmly in the wider literary context of the twentieth century."[18] More recently, scholars such as Anna Vaninskaya and Patchen Mortimer have attempted to put Tolkien in conversation with movements and figures of his own era, but as Vaninskaya observes, this has been an uphill task. She writes, "Nobody needs convincing of the presence of Anglo-Saxon and Old Norse elements in *The Lord of the Rings*, but an assertion of a similar

---

[16] Ordway, *Tolkien's Modern Reading*, 26.

[17] Ibid., 26.

[18] Ibid., 278.

kind with regard to the twentieth century still meets with suspicion."[19] Mortimer argues that Tolkien's "work reveals modernist attributes — and even ambitions of modernist scope — that deserve to be explored" but laments the prevailing "tendency to consider Tolkien's works escapist and romantic, the work of a man removed from his own time."[20] In a post-Carpenter, pre-*TMR* landscape, critics were handicapped by this myopic view, the "image of Tolkien as irredeemably anti-modern" which according to Ordway's diagnosis stems from a "too-frequent disregard of context and chronology."[21] Her remedy is as simple and effective as it is elegantly carried out: identify sources, influences, and influences-by-opposition from the nineteenth and twentieth centuries and establish their connection with the Legendarium. Thus Ordway not only busts the myth regarding Tolkien as an anti-modern medievalist, she also resets the context

---

[19] Anna Vaninskaya, "Tolkien: A Man of His Time?" in *Tolkien and Modernity 1*, ed. Frank Weinreich and Thomas Honegger (Zollikofen, Switzerland: Walking Tree, 2006), 3.

[20] Patchen Mortimer, "Tolkien and Modernism", in *Tolkien Studies,* Volume 2, (Morgantown, WV: West Virginia University Press, 2005), 113. In Mortimer's view, the Legendarium is a project "as grand and avant-garde as those of Wagner or the Futurists . . . as suffused with the spirit of the age as any by Eliot, Joyce, or Hemingway."

[21] Ordway, *Tolkien's Modern Reading*, 15.

for any future appraisal of Tolkien. If myth-busting is her first major accomplishment, then that is her second achievement, for *TMR* demonstrates convincingly that such a reappraisal is warranted, and scholars can now proceed unfettered by the distorting influence of Carpenter, et al.

As a more complete picture of Tolkien emerges, we begin to understand the man in terms of his time and place, as someone informed not only by his interest in all things medieval, but also by the era in which he lived. After all, no author works in a vacuum, and *TMR* shows us Tolkien's creative inputs included modern works by modern authors. This validates the comparisons Wilson, Vaninskaya, Mortimer, and others have made between Tolkien's literary output and that of other moderns. It also broadens the horizon for further inquiry. For example, Tolkien's work on the Legendarium extended well beyond the second world war; therefore it is not inconceivable that critics will begin to approach him as a post-modern.[22] Certainly there are aspects of Tolkien's work that anticipate much of what we now classify under that term. Kyoko Yuasa has already made inroads in that

[22] Mortimer, "Tolkien and Modernism," 128. He hints as much in his fourth footnote.

direction with her innovative analysis of C.S. Lewis as a "Christian Postmodernist."[23] Her work might serve as a template for exploring why Tolkien's influence has extended so far into our own era as to spawn myriad derivative works across a variety of media. Seen in this light, Ordway's modest claim that her study of Tolkien's modern reading only amounts to "a relatively minor element in the total picture" when compared with "his medieval reading . . . his study of languages, his personal friendships . . . and other formative experiences" may in hindsight come to be regarded as a vast understatement.[24]

---

[23] Kyoko Yuasa, *C.S. Lewis and Christian Postmodernism: Word, Image, and Beyond*. (Eugene, OR: Wipf and Stock, 2016) See especially chapters 1 and 2 and pp. 174-179.

[24] Ordway, *Tolkien's Modern Reading*, 9.

Holly Ordway speaking on Tolkien
(Photo credit: Ryan Grube)

UNVEILING REALITY THROUGH THE IMAGINATION

Jared Zimmerer on a Strategy to Fight Meaninglessness

In her spiritual memoir, *Not God's Type,* Dr. Holly Ordway explains the process of her conversion from atheism to Catholicism. Primarily through the works of J.R.R. Tolkien and C.S. Lewis, Ordway was presented with a deeper level of meaning through the imagination that eventually led to her conversion. "I cannot imagine a world more antithetical," Ordway writes of Tolkien's Middle-earth, "to the narrowness, the self-centeredness, the pointlessness of my atheist worldview, in which meaning is at best manufactured as an ever-less-effective opiate against despair."[1] Ordway's conversion led her to meaningful academic work

[1] Holly Ordway, *Not God's Type: An Atheist Academic Lays Down Her Arms* (San Francisco: Ignatius Press, 2014), chap. 6, Digital edition.

that has become a gift to both the universities and the Church. Her keen insight into the necessity of the imagination as a primary faculty of meaning and the use of this faculty as a means of evangelization ought to be shouted from the rooftops at universities, schools, and every single church that cares for its members. In an age of scientism, rationalism, and nihilism, Dr. Ordway has presented a strategy of peeling back the muck of meaninglessness to unveil reality in all its beauty.

One of my heroes, Russell Kirk, despised the problem of living in abstractions. He felt that when the human person is removed from "the real," other persons become nothing more than an idea, and everything is reduced to its use. When removed from reality, we quickly become the arbiters of our world, and the most powerful individual will triumphs over the other pawns in the game. Sadly, the intellectual madness of the last few centuries created this reductionistic attitude. The concept of reality has become subjective and material reality nothing more than a plaything. The problem lies in the fact that because our perception of reality has become so subjective, rational arguments alone cannot convince others of what is real. What Dr. Ordway has so convincingly taught over the years is that it is through the imagination that rational argument meets the real.

Think, for example, of Ray Bradbury's work, *Dandelion Wine*. Leo Auffmann's famous happiness machine, in which fabricated dreams quickly become existential nightmares, is an attempt to live in the abstraction of happiness without anything of substance, without anything real. The machine represents man's desire to create meaning based on a shallow understanding of happiness. It aims at a world with no sadness, no emotional rollercoasters, just an abstraction of what makes us feel happy. After the disastrous results of the experiment with the machine lying in ashes, Leo's wise neighbor, Grandfather Spaulding, unveils what truly makes one happy. "You want to see the *real* happiness machine?" says Grandfather Spaulding, "The one they patented a couple thousand years ago, it still runs, not good all the time, no! but it runs. It's been here all along."[2] He then proceeds to bring Leo to the window of his own home, where he sees his children playing on the floor and his wife lovingly preparing supper. In other words, the actual happiness machine is what is most real and precious — a world

[2] Ray Bradbury, *Dandelion Wine* (New York: Bantam Books, 1964), 62.

in which love sits right alongside the risk of being hurt. And further than that, once reality is unveiled as the actual happiness machine, the world itself is imbued with wonder and intensity. As a Christian and evangelist, Ordway brilliantly explains that our world has been trying to enter the fabricated happiness machine and notions of meaning are far removed from the Gospel.

In the course she produced for the Word on Fire Institute titled *Imaginative Apologetics*, she walks the students through the problem of meaning gaps in the language we use. For example, the word God can mean very different things to different people. An atheist might hear this word and think of some big being in the sky who arbitrarily commands the world through dominance, or she might think of a being akin to the Easter bunny. As Christians, we do not believe in that god either, and Ordway makes a keen insight into the need to correct such language and meaning gaps. She states that "if we are to correct the cultural narrative, we need to identify, challenge, and correct false meanings, using our reason, and we need to generate new meanings to replace the false ones, using the imagination."[3] She

[3] Holly Ordway, *Imaginative Apologetics.* Word on Fire Institute. https://wordonfire.institute/courses/imaginative/.

points out that reason is the organ of truth, and imagination is the organ of meaning, promoting an integrated approach to evangelization. Through numerous human faculties, an evangelist unveils Christianity as the most meaningful depth of reality. She states that,

> Our Catholic faith covers all of reality, so it can't be reduced to a single argument. Instead, we see multiple aspects of our faith that, when we bring them together, show a full, true, meaningful, convincing picture of reality. So we actually see that a cumulative case is more convincing. This imaginative, integrated approach, where we have both imagination and reason, is actually more compelling because it involves all of our faculties: our reason, our imagination, our emotions, our experiences.[4]

This style of meaning-making, what John Henry Newman calls real and notional apprehension, yet in an active evangelical mode, is the style the Christian church needs to focus on today.

Dr. Ordway reminds us, especially as Christians, that through wonder, assisted by the great fairy tales or beautiful images, we come to see, really see,

[4] Ordway, *Imaginative Apologetics.*

what is right in front of us. Through the imagination, a bird is not just a group of bones and sinews; it is a great messenger, a singer of God's majesty, an example of man's desire to soar the heavens. In the same way, many today view Christ as nothing more than a great teacher or a softy with a heart for the downtrodden. Through the great works of imagination, we can experience a deeper sense of the reality that is Jesus Christ. And in doing so, we remove the blindness of those around us and help them see reality as it is because Jesus Christ is the deepest sense of reality. Through Aragorn, Gandalf, and Frodo, we come to experience in a real way, Christ as king, suffering servant, and wise man. Through Aslan, we come to know Christ as dangerous, majestic, and sacrificial. If our descriptions of Christ as Messiah fails to reach the modern mind, it is because the modern imagination fails to interpret that term with meaning. As Ordway explains, "Images and metaphors are ways of communicating the truth, through the imagination, which allows for more meaning to be generated, making that truth concrete, graspable, memorable—not just abstract and easily forgotten."[5] By cultivating the imagination, an

[5] Ordway, *Imaginative Apologetics.*

evangelist imitates Grandfather Spaulding's wisdom.

The modern West is suffering from a lack of purpose and meaning. We have placed ourselves in the happiness machine by way of scientism, rationalism, and nihilism. Those with the wisdom of truth, as Kirk states, "look upward from this place of slime, this world of gorgons and chimeras, toward the light which gives Love to this poor earth and all the stars."[6] The human heart cannot help but seek meaning, but very few know where to find it. Dr. Ordway, whom I am honored to work with and call a friend, is just the warrior we need to unveil the real. It's as if she is standing at the edge of a thick forest, sword in hand, inviting mankind to follow her as she hacks away the brush, fights off the dragons of our self-interest, and unveils the sun.

---

[6] Russell Kirk, *Prospects for Conservatives* (1956; New York: Imaginative Conservative Books, 2013), 21.

(Photo credit: Ryan Grube)

"Maps," My Map

Jesse W. Baker on the Importance of Poetry

During the Apologetics Research and Writing class I took and Dr. Ordway taught, the class was assigned her book *Apologetics and the Christian Imagination*. Though each chapter concluded with a poem, my initial reaction was to skip the poems, as I doubted my ability to comprehend them. I ultimately reconsidered. Dr. Ordway's poem "Maps" particularly jumped out to me as a piece of writing that was both accessible and powerful. While there were other influences since then, "Maps" stands out as one major reason — if not the major reason — I really discovered the power of poetry. This poem is an expression of gratitude for Dr. Ordway for opening my eyes to a new way of seeing. In a sense, her poem "Maps" was a map for me, leading me into a world of poetry. I followed her sonnet format to help me describe my original misunderstanding of poetry, my later abandonment of it, and my current love for it.

"Maps," My Map

I once feigned an interest in poetry,
More as an opportunity to write
Down my feelings in some odd looking form,
Never really looking beyond myself.
Later I was focused solely on prose,
Striving for the precise, unambiguous.
Certain this was the only way one should
Seek to awaken a slumbering world.

"Maps" invited me on a different path,
Beyond feelings, and mere statement of fact.
Not just to awaken, but to enchant,
To see heaven in the ordinary.
"Maps": My first step on a poetic road
Where wonder grows deeper, the farther I go.

Poetry as Prayer, Imagination the Spark to Worship and Service:

Ordway's Review of Gerard Manley Hopkins in Word on Fire's *Ignatian Collection*

Seth Myers on Contemplation, Poetry, and Missionizing

"The world is charged with the grandeur of God.
It will flame out, like shining from shook foil"[1]

- Gerard Manley Hopkins, God's Grandeur

Holly Ordway shows her commitment to the craft of imagination as a tool for one's devotion to God in her contribution to the Word on Fire Classics 2020 *Ignatian Collection.* Ordway reviews the work of poet-priest Gerard Manley Hopkins (1844 – 1899), whose poems, though not published until nearly

[1] Gerard Manley Hopkins, "God's Grandeur" in *Ignatian Collection* (Park Ridge, IL: Word on Fire Press, 2020), 163.

twenty years after his death, established him as one of the premier poets of the Victorian era. Hopkins's poems not only celebrate God's glory imbued throughout creation, but also explore human "suffering and darkness . . . [which] made his voice more significant to the generation that had endured the First World War."[2] Ordway provides insightful guidance and commentary on over thirty of Hopkins' poems. Well-known works such as *God's Grandeur, As Kingfishers Catch Fire, Carrion Comfort*, and *Pied Beauty*, are supplemented by such poems as *The Windhover, Spring and Fall*, and *The Wreck of the Deutschland* (thirty-five stanzas on the five Franciscan nuns who drowned in 1875). Inasmuch as Hopkins was a talented poet turned Jesuit priest and struggled for a time between the two callings, his poetry illustrates the point of the *Spiritual Exercises* of Ignatius, founder of the Jesuit order, in their contemplation of Christ's calling as a model for our own.

The *Ignatian Collection* provides a threefold perspective on discerning one's spiritual calling by examining the writings of three Jesuit priests: Society of Jesus founder Ignatius of Loyola (1491 –

---

[2] Holly Ordway, "Introduction to Selected Poems of Gerard Manley Hopkins" in *Ignatian Collection* (Park Ridge, IL: Word on Fire Press, 2020), 163.

1566); Ignatius's colleague Francis Xavier (1506 – 1552), a priest turned missionary to India, Japan, and China; and poet-priest Gerard Manley Hopkins (1844 – 1899). All three were adventurers in their own way: Ignatius pursued an ambitious military career until cannonball wounds to his legs led him to devote himself instead to Christ and the church, after scoring "Firsts" in his Oxford examinations, Hopkins forsook a promising academic career for the life of a Jesuit priest and poet, and Francis Xavier applied the Ignatian disciplines as a missionary to India, Japan, and China. The collection captures the spirit of Ignatius, "restless, moving ever-onward, unsatisfied with the quality of his relationship with the Lord, always convinced that the divine love could be answered by a more expansive fidelity on his part."[3]

Bishop Robert Barron likens Ignatius's *Exercises* to such landmark literature as the *Summa Theologica* of Thomas Aquinas or the *Divine Comedy* of Dante, noting the distinct call of Ignatius's work to be practiced rather than merely read. The *Spiritual Exercises* of Ignatius of Loyola commence the volume, just as Ignatius and a band of friends

---

[3] Bishop Robert Barron, "Introduction to *The Spiritual Exercises*" in *Ignatian Collection* (Park Ridge, IL: Word on Fire, 2020), 3.

founded the Jesuit order in 1534, taking vows of poverty and chastity in the service of Christ. The exercises are comprised of four weeks of meditation, beginning with an examination of one's conscience, followed by a focus on the life of Christ, on the passion week of Christ, and on the resurrection of Christ. The exercises have guided Jesuits for five hundred years, and the translation given improves the clarity from previous editions.[4]

While the exercises of Ignatius help us focus our call to worship and serve God, it is in the poetry of Hopkins that we find the many clues hidden in nature of the character of this God we are to worship. Hopkins's poetry also illustrates the same spiritual struggle for which Ignatius designed his exercises to serve as a guide. Hopkins's poetic skill is elucidated by Ordway as she explains how the "sprung rhythm" of his meter and his use of the fourteen-line Petrarchan sonnet help him to explore "small, intensely focused scenes or ideas."[5] Further Hopkins is unafraid to invent words to convey meaning, Ordway notes. For instance, in his "Spring

[4] Translation provided by Louis J. Puhl, SJ of the Pontifical College Josephinum, Worthington, Ohio. Puhl explains that this new English translation incorporates a more idiomatic than literal translation from Ignatius's original Spanish version.

[5] Holly Ordway, "Introduction to Selected Poems of Gerard Manley Hopkins," 164.

and Fall" poem, in the line, "Margaret, are you grieving / Over Goldengrove unleaving?" the word "unleaving" portrays Autumn "as a reversal of the trees' springtime life;" this mood is further evoked in the description of "worlds of wanwood leafmeal," as the sadness of "wan" and fragmentation of "meal" (as in "piecemeal") reinforce the unleafing of Autumn.[6] Hopkins then connects this grieving of the seasons to human grief in the final couplet with, "It is the blight man was born for, / It is Margaret you mourn for."[7] In a few brief lines, Hopkins depicts the decay and death unleashed by sin, and the toll it takes on humanity. It is to other poems that we must now turn to see Hopkins's depiction of God.

"The Windhover" sonnet shows how Hopkins draws on creation to illustrate the nature of it. Describing a kestrel, a small type of falcon which hovers before diving to hunt, Hopkins shows Christ as not the "domesticated, undemanding, unthreatening" Lamb of God — "Hopkins will have none of that" Ordway declares — but as a princely and even knightly bird, a "chevalier" and "daylight's

---

[6] Holly Ordway, "Introduction to Selected Poems of Gerard Manley Hopkins," 165.

[7] Ibid.

dauphin" replete with a kingdom.[8] Like Aslan, of whom Mr. Beaver declares "He's wild, you know" and "not like a *tame* lion," or like the "Dove descending" which "breaks the air / With flame of incandescent terror," an image of seemingly contradictory aspects of the Holy Spirit in T.S Eliot's "Four Quartets," so is the Christly kestrel "lovely" but also "dangerous."[9] [10]

"Brute beauty and valour and act,
oh, air, pride, plume

AND the fire that breaks from thee
then, a billion

Times lovelier, more dangerous, O
my chevalier!"[11]

Hopkins further illustrates the nature of God, in its surprising if not paradoxical range, in his well-

---

[8] Holly Ordway, "Introduction to Selected Poems of Gerard Manley Hopkins," 167.

[9] C.S. Lewis, *The Lion, the Witch and the Wardrobe* (New York: Collier Books, 1977), 180.

[10] T.S. Eliot, "Little Gidding" IV in *T.S. Eliot The Complete Poems and Plays: 1909 - 1950* (NewYork: Harcourt, Brace & Jovanovich, 1971), 143. The imagery is suggestive of a wartime bomber, a phenomenon known all too well by Eliot's World War II era British audience.

[11] Hopkins, "The Windhover" in *Ignatian Collection*, 193.

known poem "Pied Beauty." The ode's opening intent of declaring "Glory be to God" is attested by both the whimsical, "dappled things" and "skies of colour as a brinded cow," and the mundane, the patchwork of "landscape plotted and pieced" and "all trades" with their "tackle and trim."[12] Ordway concludes by explaining how the final lines, "He fathers forth whose beauty is past change: / Praise Him," show God as "not the distant Watchmaker of deism, nor the impersonal nature-force of pantheism, nor yet the random chance at work of naturalism, but the Father, who is active in the world here and now."[13]

The struggle of heeding the call to follow Christ is seen in six sonnets of desolation (as they are known) of Hopkins included in the collection, including such works as "Carrion Comfort," "Patience," and "No worst, there is none." These poems align with the introspective part of Ignatius's exercises, and can serve as a devotional supplement to them. Lines such as "O the mind, mind had mountains; cliffs of fall / Frightful, sheer, no-man-fathomed. Hold them cheap / May who ne'er hung

---

[12] Hopkins, "Pied Beauty" in *Ignatian Collection*, 211.

[13] Ordway, "Introduction to Selected Poems of Gerard Manley Hopkins," in *Ignatian Collection*, 169.

there"[14] voice despair but also point to Christ who suffered for us.

Ordway provides helpful notes for all the poems included, and her selections and commentary reinforce the point of the Ignatian exercises, that we should behold the glory of God and so align our life's calling. She advises that deeper observations from many of the poems will not surface on the first, second, or even fifth readings; the "astonishing body of poetry" created by Hopkins "is a gift for all readers, who can learn much about prayer in his school of poetry."[15]

The final section of the *Ignatian Collection*, collected letters from Jesuit priest turned missionary Francis Xavier, reinforces the call to service as inspired by the devotional works of Ignatius and Hopkins. Francis's call to service, as it follows Ignatius's contemplation of Christ's challenge to us, and Hopkins's poetic show of the divine in nature, is reminiscent of Dorothy Sayers's triadic modeling of the creative work of the divine artist in *The Mind of the Maker*.[16] Just as Sayers casts

---

[14] Hopkins, "No worst, there is none" in *Ignatian Collection*, 199.

[15] Ibid.,174.

[16] Dorothy Sayers, *The Mind of the Maker* (San Francisco: HarperSanFrancisco, 1987).

God the Father as the original, inspiring *idea*, Jesus as the incarnate *energy*, and the Holy Spirit as the animating *power* of God's work in the world, the triad of Ignatius, Hopkins, and Francis exhibit an analogous movement from contemplation to incarnation to service. Ignatius's spiritual exercise leads us to contemplation of the divine source or *idea*, Hopkins's poetry incarnates the *energy* of God in the world, and the mission work of Francis shows the *power* of God's redemption at work in the world.

Francis, as much the pioneer as Ignatius, declared how futile a life of complete contemplation could be. In a letter to Ignatius, he implored for missions workers:

> There is now in these parts a very large number of persons who have only one reason for not becoming Christian, and that is that there is no one to make them Christians. It often comes into my mind to go round all the Universities of Europe, and especially that of Paris, crying out everywhere like a madman, and saying to all the learned men there whose learning is so much greater than their charity, "Ah! What a multitude of souls is through your fault shut out of heaven and falling into hell!" Would to God that these men who labor so much in gaining knowledge would give as much thought to the

> account they must one day give to God of the use they have made of their learning and of the talents entrusted to them![17]

Despite his plea against the excess of knowledge, it was through teaching the doctrines of the Christian faith that he impacted tens of thousands of souls in India and Japan; he died while waiting to be smuggled into China. In India, Francis would first preach to the idle and the young, using songs and jingles (music, like Hopkins's poetry, an imaginative art) at times mixed with doctrines, then move onto adult audiences. Ten of Francis's letters to Ignatius are included, describing his work in India and Japan, and his plans for China. Besides reports of the work in general, Francis offers insights into methods of engaging the imagination of Indian, Japanese and Chinese minds. In India, provincial leaders could allow or discourage Christian faith, though answered prayers were often effective for the cause of faith; such incarnations of the work of God in the lives of Indians parallel Hopkins's poetic illuminations of the divine in nature. Nevertheless, just as C.S. Lewis warned that "it must not be supposed that I am in any sense putting for the

[17] Francis Xavier, "Letter to the Society at Rome," Dec. 31, 1542, in *Ignatian Collection*, 313.

imagination as the organ of truth" — "reason is the natural organ of truth; but imagination is the organ of meaning" — so did Francis's engagement with Hindus involve matters of doctrinal truth.[18] Even though Brahmins believed in a single God, Francis claimed that they encouraged idol worship to keep power and to exact offerings. In lieu of a Christian doctrine and story of redemption, Brahmin principles were just two: enforcing worship of cows and reverence for the Brahmins, who alone worshipped the gods (idols were in fact images of devils). Francis thus countered these with the Apostles's Creed, the Ten Commandments, and the basic doctrines of heaven and hell. Despite many Brahmins declaring their admiration of the truth of Christian doctrines, they yet resisted conversion due to social pressure and the risk of their Brahmin livelihood; Francis spoke also of the "intensity and abundance of the joy of God" given to those at labor in His fields of harvest.[19] Francis's work shows how the imagination, by way of the arts, can serve the

---

[18] C.S. Lewis, "Bluspels and Falansferes" in *Selected Literary Essays*, ed. Walter Hooper (Cambridge: Cambridge University Press, 2013), 265. Also online pseudepigraph.us/wp-content/uploads/2015/07/CSL-Bluspels-and-Flalansferes.pdf.

[19] Lewis, "Bluspels and Falansferes" in *Selected Literary Essays*, 319.

cause of the gospel, though it must be allied with doctrinal truth.

Francis's missionary work in Japan demonstrated even more strongly the need for imaginative engagement with pagan cultures. After ministry in the state of Goa in India as well as the islands of Malacca, Francis next considered the nations of Japan and China. The Japanese popular imagination, like that of India, was subject to the power and traditions of their own cultural elites, whether political or scholarly. Missionaries needed "the most remarkable strength of soul and patience" as they faced "the whole glory and reputation of a haughty people relying on its pride and its institutions;" "their boldness will expose them to a thousand sufferings when the hornets they have irritated shall fly upon them."[20] Francis's assessment affirms not just the call of Ignatian exercises to self-denial and taking up the cross of Christ, but also the importance of Hopkins's poetic work. Hopkins's scholarly sonnets vie with those of the native intellectual elites (the Japanese being well-known for their own nature poetry), the divine beauty that Hopkins finds rivalling the more

[20] Francis Xavier, "Letter to my holy Father in Jesus Christ, Ignatius at Rome," Jan. 29, 1552 in *Ignatian Collection*, 345.

naturalistic bent of Japanese aesthetics.[21] Nevertheless, as in his ministry with Hindus, issues of doctrine were important as well. Francis called for missionaries to Japan to be philosophically adept to show the flaws in their typically Buddhist- and Shinto-leaning doctrines. Francis's letters were prescient, as he would later make headway into Japan by showing the parallels between Shinto and Christian terms of worship, though Japan would soon turn to persecution of Christians after he left. Francis died while waiting to travel to China, though since he felt that it was the source of the Japanese religions, one suspects his approach there would have been similar to that in his work in Japan.

In her discussion of the poetry of Hopkins, Ordway shows the role of the imagination to be vital in how we comprehend God. The imagination is fundamental in the exercises of Ignatius as we measure our introspections by the figure of Christ, as well as in the missionary work of Francis in engaging and enlightening the non-Christian mind.

---

[21] The Eastern aesthetic emphasis on harmony in nature rather than transcendence is discussed in F.S.C. Northrop's *The Meeting of East and West* (New York: Collier, 1946). Christian artist and writer Makoto Fujimura discusses Japanese aesthetics and hints of Christian transcendence therein in *Silence and Beauty: Hidden Faith Born of Suffering* (Downers Grove: IVP Press, 2017), including a foreword by Philip Yancey.

Ordway's work on Hopkins is in the center of this triad of contemplation to calling, poetry as prayer, and the missionizing work of correcting misled imaginations.

Some Real Magic: Taliessin Lectureth in the School of the Poets

Donald T. Williams on the Poetic Imagination

Within the cadences of human speech
    Attentive listeners can sometimes hear
    The rhythm of the wave upon the beach
    Or listen to the music of the spheres.
Within the small sphere of the human eye
    The watcher who knows how to look can see
    A spirit that's as lofty as the sky
    Or humble as the lover on his knee.

When in the alembic of the human mind
    Imagination boils with memory,
    Such vision with such sound can be combined,
    Far more mysterious than alchemy!
The Philosopher's Stone we vainly sought of old
    Could never have made such rare and costly gold.

From Stars through the Clouds: The Collected Poetry of Donald T. Williams, 2n edition (Lantern Hollow Press, 2020). Used by permission.

A Case of Mistaken Identity

Jason M. Smith on Our Great Misconception

I said to my soul, be still, and let the dark come upon you
Which shall be the darkness of God.

- T.S. Eliot, "East Coker"

I fancied myself chased by hounds of Hell, and fled.

But as I fled, I reasoned: what want of hounds has Hell?
Hell is everywhere. It needs neither quarry nor guard; they that remain
Themselves harry back from the chapel in its gates; they that escape, escape beyond Hell's hope.

So I knew them for hounds of God, and that was worse.

It was springtide, and I fled the flooding *Dao*

The river's rush-and-tumble, revel and revelation
Of headwaters. That bright current
Dooms the devout to exhaustion or else, against instinct,
To bruised, broken, bloodied surrender.

And I heard my lover's voice, calling for me.

From love, then, I fled: love, self's best betrayal,
Love, the undying crucifixion
Suicide's obverse, all in its consummation
Love consumes.

But however I fled, ever closer I heard them come:
Barking dogs, swift-coursing babble, love
That knew me already by name.

I jerked, thrashed, screamed in the void where no words are,
No sound, no friction, no space
Still they closed upon me.

At the moment of utmost horror, my eyes
Opened: I sat on a bright field
With dogs playing all about me. Insensate,
I had been engaged in their happy romp

As they bounded across my lap or pushed noses
under my unfeeling palms
Whether I knew or not, whether I would or no.
The sensation of their pursuit had been
A trick of my own ears, slow to hear,
And of my mind, slow to wake. I had been at bay
From the beginning.

Gloss

Two books accompanied me to the car dealership that day: Holly Ordway's *Not God's Type* (the first edition, with the goldfish on the cover), which I was finishing; and C.S. Lewis's *The Great Divorce*, which I was starting.

An acquaintance had put Ordway's memoir literally into my hands — after overhearing me describe what I was then calling the "veiled apologetic" in my fantasy novel series *Fayborn*. He interrupted his own conversation at the next table to swivel his chair around and interrupt mine. "You need to meet Holly Ordway," he said. "Apologetics and the imagination — that's what she does!" Next week, he brought me *Not God's Type*, which he traded for a promise of safe return. "It's not in print right now," he explained. "Irreplaceable."

My car's airbag was part of a recall, and I was stuck at the service center, waiting. At a wooden picnic table in the parking lot I poured through the final pages of Ordway's story, compelled not by any mystery around *what* would happen but *when*, and *how*, and *why*. I remember pacing around the table at the conclusion, processing through energy and excitement, before picking up *The Great Divorce*.

It would have been my second time through *The Great Divorce*, but I got no farther than the Preface — arrested by a curious line in which Lewis proposes that Earth "will not be found by anyone to be a very distinct place." Here is its context:

> I do not think that all who choose wrong roads perish; but their rescue consists in being put back on the right road. A wrong sum can be put right: but only by going back till you find the error and working it afresh from that point, never by simply going on. Evil can be undone, but it cannot "develop" into good . . . If we insist on keeping Hell (or even earth) we shall not see Heaven: if we accept Heaven we shall not be able to retain even the smallest and most intimate souvenirs of Hell. I believe, to be sure, that any man who reaches Heaven will find that what he abandoned (even in plucking out his right eye) was precisely nothing: that the kernel of what he was really seeking even in his most

> depraved wishes will be there, beyond expectation, waiting for him in "the High Countries." In that sense it will be true for those who have completed the journey (and for no others) to say that good is everything and Heaven everywhere. But we, at this end of the road, must not try to anticipate that retrospective vision. If we do, we are likely to embrace the false and disastrous converse and fancy that everything is good and everywhere is Heaven.
>
> But what, you ask, of earth? Earth, I think, will not be found by anyone to be in the end a very distinct place. I think earth, if chosen instead of Heaven, will turn out to have been, all along, only a region in Hell: and earth, if put second to Heaven, to have been from the beginning a part of Heaven itself.[1]

In view of Ordway's testimony, these words struck home like lightning. I seized pad and pen and scribbled out (more or less) the poem you have just read. For it is not about Earth that we in our rebellious state are primarily mistaken, but rather, as *The Great Divorce* shows in example after example, we are mistaken about ourselves. The

---

[1] C.S. Lewis, *The Great Divorce* (New York: HarperOne, 2001), viii-ix.

great mistake does not consist solely of conceiving of Earth as a "distinct place," but fundamentally in conceiving of Myself as a Distinct Person. Both fantasies are scarcely true. A rebellious soul is lapsing toward nothingness, increasingly unreal, increasingly unable to recognize reality. As *The Great Divorce*'s MacDonald puts it, we rebels are "Grumblers" gradually disappearing until only a "Grumble" remains. Because we are wrong about ourselves, we can't help but be wrong about . . . everything else.

Notes

Title: Paired with the first-person narrative, "A Case of Mistaken Identity" suggests that the poem's genre is a detective story. The poem sets up this expectation and subverts it twice. First, in detective stories the reader is accustomed to relying on the narrator for an objective view into the facts and events of the case. Here, the poem relies instead on the Untrustworthy Narrator trope to set up its turn. Second, in first-person detective stories the narrator is usually the sleuth or sleuth's companion, solving the case or at least contributing to its resolution. Here, the narrator progressively realizes his powerlessness and awakens in the nightmarish moment just before death, only to realize that the case had long been resolved — and that he was the last to know.

Epigraph: "East Coker" is particularly invoked in the 8th stanza.

"I reasoned": Ordway and Lewis both were greatly persuaded by reason and rational argument and engaged by believing friends to reconsider their positions on God and Christianity. "'Come now, let us reason together,' says the Lord." (Isaiah 1:8)

"the chapel in its gates": On rare occasions when I have heard preachers address Matthew 16:18, they have spoken of the Church as if it were a battering ram or some other siege weapon that the closed gates of Hell are unable to resist. This picture, I think, confuses the grammar of Christ's statement (of the two nouns, Hell's gates is the thing acting, not the Church) and confuses the sequence of events (Christ's harrowing of Hell occurs before the Church is founded; see Eph. 4:8-10, 1 Pet. 4:6). Here the poem implies a more Lewisian image: though Christ has already opened the gates of Hell, the self-damned keep on trying to close them again; a chapel, placed as a doorstop to prevent the gates from closing, creates the egress through which the penitent can freely escape.[2]

"Hell's hope": "The mind is its own place, and in itself / Can make a Heav'n of Hell, a Hell of Heav'n. / What matter where, *if I be still the same . . .* / Better to reign in Hell, then serve in Heav'n" (*Paradise Lost*, Book I, *emphasis added*).

"hounds of God": This poem's central image is indebted to Francis Thompson's 1893 poem "The Hound of Heaven."

"that was worse": The narrator would rather be caught by Hell-hounds than by God, baldly revealing his perspective. "Amiable agnostics will talk cheerfully about 'man's search for God.' To me, as I then was, they might as well have talked about the mouse's search for the cat . . . I had always wanted, above all things, not to be 'interfered with.' I had wanted (mad wish) 'to call my soul my own.'"[3]

---

[2] Compare Lewis's speculations about Hell and its willing occupants in *The Great Divorce*, *The Problem of Pain*, and *Mere Christianity*.

[3] C.S. Lewis, *Surprised by Joy* (New York: Mariner Books, 2012), 227-8.

Dao: This word (formerly more often anglicized as *Tao*) and the experiences and argument of this stanza will be familiar to readers of *The Abolition of Man* and *Mere Christianity* Book 1: "Right and Wrong as a Clue to the Meaning of the Universe." See also Romans 7: "If it had not been for the law, I would not have known sin."

"obverse": This word implies that the untrustworthy narrator sees love and suicide as two sides of the same coin. He gets that love consists of self-sacrifice or self-denial for the beloved's sake . . . and has no interest in taking part.

"however I fled": *c.f.* Psalm 139.

"babble": Words like this reinforce the narrator's incapacity to truly understand what is pursuing him and what he is being offered.

"in the void": A calculated retreat from God is, ultimately, a retreat into Nothingness and inagency. Without realizing or acknowledging it, the self-damned will the loss of their will — and eventually, according to *The Great Divorce* and *The Problem of Pain*, they get what they want.

“engaged in their happy romp”: That God pursues us for our own good, for in fact the only real and lasting good we can possibly experience, is incomprehensible foolishness to the soul in rebellion and astonishing to the rebel soul when finally glimpsed. This is the truth one must first believe in order to see. “O taste and see that the Lord is good!” (Psalm 34:8) There is no greater proof of God’s greatness than his glory and stature being undiminished, even magnified, by his undignified and delighted pursuit of a stubborn and rebellious people.

“at bay / From the beginning”: Surrendering to God feels like the loss of everything when we finally face that choice. But then, looking back from the other side, we see clearly that we had nothing, and so lost nothing. Choosing not to lay down arms (what arms?) is futile, if God were not meek. A soul that continues in rebellion is a babe in its mother’s womb, demanding not to be born. Yet if we consent to our fingers being pried from the nothingness to which we cling, we begin, and continue into joy.

Jason Smith writes poetry and fiction under the pen name J. Aleksandr Wootton. "A Case of Mistaken Identity" is slated to appear in his sophomore collection, due out soon. His first collection, Muninn Wandering, *is currently available from most major online bookstores.*

THE CHALLENGE OF "THE REPUBLIC"

Donald T. Williams on What Ought to Be

Plato banned the Poets from his state,
    Yet said, if one could make a sound defense
    In lilting verse with cogent arguments
That they do more than merely imitate
An imitation and dissimulate,
    He'd take them back again. And ever since
    Our best minds have been trying to convince
His cautious Guardians of their mistake.

Sir Philip Sidney laid a firm foundation

    In his divine "Defense of Poesy":

The Poet gives us Virtue's exaltation

    More strong than History or Philosophy,

Concretely shows through his imagination

    Not just what is, but more: what ought to be.

From Stars through the Clouds: The Collected Poetry of Donald T. Williams, 2nd edition (Lantern Hollow Press, 2020). Used by permission.

Carry On

Donald W.Catchings, Jr. on the Teacher's Call

Like bells of Rivendell ring (They sing! They sing!),
Her song, it summons hungry hearts to hear.
Harken your ear. A sudden goldfinch rings
With songs of grace — its piercing love and care.
Harken! I say. She can't stay long. She must
Move quick. Her wings are fire. From tree to leaf
They spread life to the dead. A holy thrust . . .
Then shrill! The Wraith is cut with wit. And grief,
The grief of fledglings, flees like dispersed chaff
In winds so fair, so fast they free, at last,
The burdened hearts. Now in mirth, we all laugh,
"The bird's moved on." (We remember the past.)
Her first and final note, a lasting song.
With Angelus toll, the Teacher calls — Carry on!

Learning Writing at Writespace

Jamie Danielle Portwood on the Importance of Community

I met Dr. Holly Ordway and Writespace on the same day, at HBU's 2015 Spring Writers' Conference. I was new to Houston and my friend had invited me to come with her as she knew I was trying to be a writer. At the conference, I took a flyer about upcoming workshops at a little literary arts organization called Writespace and I took a workshop on memoir since I was working on a memoir. Actually, it felt more like banging my head against a memoir, but my friend was game so we sat ourselves in the front seats at Dr. Holly Ordway's workshop on writing memoir.

I remember the conversation my friend and I were having. I had announced that one should never say never as God surely considers it a dare.

"I mean, here I am in Houston after swearing I would never live in Texas. I swore it on nearly every one of those 879 miles of I-10 that exist in the state of Texas on the drive between my mom in Florida and college in Arizona."

There was a flash of humor and kindred spirit from Dr. Ordway as she laughed and winked at me. "Oh is that ever true! Remind me to tell you how a former atheist turned Christian converted to Catholicism while teaching at a Baptist university." I knew I was in for a good workshop because a teacher who can laugh is one I know I will love.

That workshop in 2015 was only an hour. Honestly, I don't even remember what she taught about memoir. But in 2016, when I took on the job as workshop coordinator at Writespace and we needed a memoir instructor, I wanted Dr. Ordway.

I wanted her particularly because she is one of those teachers who not only loves to teach but is also permanently curious and passionate about the subject they are teaching. That kind of passion and energy are contagious and I wanted to have each student come away from a Writespace workshop filled with new energy.

It's why I always ask instructors if there is a subject they are particularly geeked to teach. Given the fact that she is one of the world's foremost Tolkien and Lewis scholars, I was not at all surprised that both were a part of her pitch. I *was* surprised that it wasn't a memoir workshop.

Collaboration and Creativity was a workshop that used the Inklings to illustrate how important community is for a writer, especially for writers engaged in long-term writing projects. For some reason, I took the trope of the melancholy, starving artist too seriously. I had this idea that writing had to be done alone — that it was supposed to be hard and lonely. Learning from Dr. Ordway that Tolkien — and understand, I read *The Lord of the Rings* once a year — that Lewis — *The Chronicles of Narnia* are almost memorized because I read them *at least* once a year — hung out regularly over pints in the local pub and collaborated creatively changed the landscape of writing for me. Her workshop gave me permission to seek out a community to write in. Being a part of a writing community changed everything for me.

I mean, I still haven't finished my memoir, but I haven't thrown the whole thing out altogether either. The writerly friends I found believe in my memoir when I am so discouraged I have given up believing in it myself. I've done the same for them. We keep each other going the same way that the Inklings did.

Dr. Ordway's Visual Guide to Paragraph Structure

Josiah Peterson on Creating Meaning

While it may not be among her best known works — yet — Dr. Ordway's "Visual Guide to Paragraph Structure" garners instant recognition and nostalgic nods of appreciation from alumni of her Research Writing and Apologetics class. The guide pithily and visually explains the purpose and structure of paragraphs along with guidance for recognizing and avoiding common pitfalls and strategies for editing essays in light of paragraphs. One student I shared it with told me she learned more from the guide than a semester of college writing. A couple HBU alumni (this author being one) are in the early stages of working with Holly Ordway to make it into a short book, complete with updated visuals, sample paragraphs, and an introduction with advice on how instructors might best use the guide. Apart from expressing gratitude and admiration for Holly Ordway in a journal issue dedicated to her work, the Paragraph Guide is worthy of attention to cultural apologists for how it helps Christians fulfill God's creative and missional calling.

"Be fruitful and multiply, fill the earth and subdue it." In the context of Genesis 1, God's command to Adam and Eve most directly refers to raising children, cultivating and ruling the earth, but the implications extend to all creative outputs of the creatures made in the image of a creator God.

Including words. God created through words. God assigned Adam the task of naming animals. Adam creates poetry when he first sees Eve (Gen 2:23). God calls his prophets to speak his word and the great commission is to go into all the world and preach the gospel. Producing good and beautiful words is an innately human, God-ordained endeavor.

Paragraphs, as Dr. Ordway's guide explains, are a structure for helping arrange good words. Paragraphs convey one thought, introduced in the first, "topic," sentence, and explained and supported in the rest of the paragraph. The paragraph also situates the thought in relation to the paper as a whole and to the immediately surrounding paragraphs. Visually this is an upward pointing triangle, a focused point followed by its supporting foundation. Recognizing this purpose of paragraphs unlocks their potential expression and communication. Do you have a point you want to make? Try using a paragraph.

Creativity, while part of the natural and original plan, was complicated by the fall. The earth is less naturally fruitful than it once was, and we have to work — by the sweat of our brow against the thorns and thistles — to make it productive. Childbirth is now a painful experience. The creation mandate is much harder to fulfill.

So too with words. One stares at a barren page that matches one's barren mind. At other times words spring up in an untamed jungle threatening to tangle up the unwary traveler. Some writings never make it to fruition, while the fruit of some writing ends up being sour, woody, or overly ripe.

Dr. Ordway's guide identifies many of the challenges writers encounter when writing paragraphs. The headless paragraph — a trapezoid, or triangle missing the top point — leaves the purpose of the paragraph unclear. The two-idea paragraph, usually a really long paragraph represented by a triangle within a triangle, attempts to convey separate points but fails to distinguish them, ultimately obscuring both. The "everything but the kitchen sink paragraph," which is oddly often a short paragraph, contains many potential topic sentences that need to be split up (a jagged-edged polygon). The "floaty" paragraph — round circles — might go anywhere but fit nowhere.

Ordway not only identifies common problems, she advises on how to solve them. Look to the end of the paragraph to see if you have a summative statement that may serve as a topic sentence. Look for transition words like "although" or "so" and consider starting a new paragraph. Ask "what is this paragraph about?" write the answer, and if it fits the essay, use it as a topic sentence. If it doesn't, cut the paragraph (perhaps saving the idea for a future essay). Ordway's advice provides guidance for plowing fields and pruning jungles.

As with words, Ordway's guide is not only meant to benefit the creator, but is ultimately meant to benefit the recipient of the creation. The fruit of the garden is not just for the grower, nor the jungle path only for the first explorer. The writing process in particular should be other-oriented as the goal is to create meaning for the reader. Insofar as writers make an effort to make their writing clear and compelling, their writing is a labor of love.

Dr. Ordway's "Visual Guide to Paragraph Structure" is the fruit of years of experience, a cultivated understanding of the joys and travails of the creative process, and a compassionate love for truth, beauty, and goodness. And this fruit carries its own seeds such that all who have tasted it want to see it spread.

Lost and Found

Theresa Pihl on Changing Perspective

Maddie leaned against the kitchen counter and sipped her coffee: black as the grief that threatened to overwhelm her once again. A pile of dirty dishes spilled over the sink. An empty pizza box sprawled across the table. She looked past the mess out of the open window where spring sunlight streamed. She heard the sparrows chattering away, beginning their day in the eaves of her porch. She closed her eyes and breathed in the steam from her mug, absorbing the bitter smooth taste of her favorite French Roast. When she opened her eyes, she caught sight of her hand. Something was not right . . . The pearl in the ring that James had given her on their 25th wedding anniversary, the year he died, was gone! The setting prongs gaped at her like frozen talons gripping emptiness.

Frantically, she glanced around the room, but everything looked cluttered — a perfect background for the "I Spy" puzzles her kids played when they were young, but this was no game. Adrenaline evaporated the morning fog from her brain, and a sense of urgency took over. She looked at the sink. Could it have fallen off when she washed her hands? She lifted everything out of the basin and carefully checked the drain. The counters? She gathered several cups; a Diet Coke can sloshed its contents onto the linoleum floor. She grabbed a fresh dishrag out of the drawer, soaped it up, and began wiping the sticky ooze. Kneeling provided a shift in perspective and gave her a view of the hidden filth lurking in the crevice between the cupboard and the stove. "This spot mopping is not going to do the trick," she thought. She needed a plan.

Regaining her feet, she started with the garbage and sifted through the trash. The rancid smell turned her stomach; but, task completed, she tied the edges into a knot and tossed it into the bin behind the garage. She then caged the clutter: throwaway, giveaway, recycle. Counters bare, she scrubbed them down, the oven and refrigerator, too. She cleaned everything; nothing escaped her notice.

At last, with the dishes put away, the floor mopped, and a fresh breeze ruffling the curtains framing the window, she saw it: her pearl! It was on the sill behind the sink. It must have popped off when she opened the window. The breath that had caught in her throat puffed past her lips. Tears pooled, spilled, ran down her cheeks. She felt James's presence; a whisper brushed her ear. She picked up the pearl, kissed it, and held it gently in the palm of her hand. Peace washed over her. James was with God; God was with her.

Maddie resettled against the counter; a fresh cup of coffee softened with a splash of cream warmed her hands. She surveyed the bright, well-ordered space and smiled. To the birds singing outside her window she called, "Rejoice with me! I have found my lost pearl! I was lost, but now I am found."

Questions for Reflection:

1) Maddie "looks past the mess" as she sips her morning coffee, enjoying the birds outside her window. She is unmotivated to change. Are there aspects in our lives that we need to address, but ignore or simply "spot mop"?

2) Maddie discovers that kneeling provides a shift in perspective and helps her see more clearly. How might prayer help us see more clearly? How can we make it part of our "plan"?

3) Sparrows recall God's providential care.[1] Have you ever experienced an unexpected event or situation that jarred you out of your daily routine only to realize later that it opened a door creating space for an invasion of Grace?

[1] Luke 12:7

ECHO AND NARCISSUS - A MODERN REIMAGINING

Clark Weidner on the Goodness of Reality

A Note on Holly Ordway and Fiction

When I enrolled as a student at Houston Baptist University to study Christian Apologetics, I supposed I would primarily read logic or philosophy. I also mistakenly assumed that these disciplines were disconnected from the world of literature and imagination; then I met Dr. Holly Ordway. In several of her classes, we were assigned poems, stories, memoirs, and other imaginative devices in an effort to understand the power of storytelling.

One particular assignment in her class was to retell a Greek myth in a way that communicates truth or beauty effectively. After putting in hours trying to retell the story of Echo and Narcissus from a fresh angle, I turned in my assignment. As per usual, Ordway's feedback was simple and sharp. To paraphrase her, it was something to the effect of "why not modernize this story? Consider placing the characters in our world." I never forgot that suggestion, so I've revisited a classroom assignment in an attempt to take on the challenge set before me by Dr. O.

* * *

Echo and Narcissus: A Modern Reimagining

"A Narcissist! Can you believe she called me that?" Mr. Hunter asked with genuine shock. "If a man can't check his phone once in a while on a date, then no woman will want me. My phone puts food on my table, for goodness sake!"

His secretary, Mrs. Juno, wanted to tell him how rude it was to text on a first date, but, instead, she tried looking sympathetic. "You just need someone with a little more patience, Mr. Hunter. You'll find her." She was lying through her teeth. No woman could possibly put up with Mr. Hunter, for he was every bit of a narcissist. Sure, he was incredibly intelligent and about as handsome as Clark Gable, but he cared about other people like a shark cares for a herd of seals.

"You know Mr. Hunter, there's this great book I've been reading that might help with your date nights. If you want, I could . . ."

He held up a finger at Mrs. Juno as if he were shushing his own child and touched his earpiece. "Hunter Real Estate. This is Mr. Hunter speaking. Let's hunt down your next home. " He gestured to Mrs. Juno to hand him a pen, then scrambled into his office.

A few minutes later the intercom buzzed: "Mrs. Juno. What's this device on my desk? It greeted me by name when I came in the door. The thing creeped me out."

"Sorry, Mr. Hunter," she said. "I meant to tell you about that. The device is called an Echo. It's an interactive device that can set all of your appointments, answer questions, and it can even play music upon request." She smiled as if she were waiting on a "thank you." Or perhaps "this is really nice."

Instead, Mr. Hunter responded, "But Mrs. Juno, that's what I pay *you* for. Except this thing can even sing and dance for me. You're not trying to quit on me are you?" It was a joke, of course, but given his current track record with women, it didn't feel entirely out of the question.

"No, Mr. Hunter. Not at all! I only thought this might help organize your busy schedule. I'll still be here to help you with plenty of other things." She sighed and then added, "At any rate, this was my husband's newest gadget. He was spending a little too much time with it, so I talked him into giving it away." She felt her cheeks reddening as she began to consider that he didn't find her gift amusing.

After some painful silence on the intercom she thought to say, "By the way. To use it you have to call out to it. It will reply if and when you say the word, '*echo*'."

"Very well," said Mr. Hunter, and he hung up the line. Mrs. Juno put her face in her hands thinking this had been a terrible idea.

Inside his office, Mr. Hunter stood staring down at the device for a few seconds. "Um . . ." he said, touching the square with his index finger as if he expected a genie to apparate from a lamp. "Hi *Echo*."

Without a moment's hesitation, the machine blinked, "Hello and good afternoon, Mr. Hunter. How may I assist you?"

For the first time since he could remember, he was impressed by something. Like a child with a sweet tooth in a candy store, Mr. Hunter then started making a long list of demands to Echo. Each time she would respond, “Task completed, Mr. Hunter. Will that be all?” And each time he added another item to the agenda.

The remainder of the workweek went by and with it, the device seemed to watch Mr. Hunter more closely every day. It became aware of his favorite foods. It knew to give him directions home sometime around six o’clock. It was the first to tell him “Happy Birthday.” It kept track of his daily caloric intake. It monitored his stock portfolio, and it even knew about his secret love of the soundtrack to *The Sound of Music*.

Within a week’s time, Mr. Hunter was so happy with the device that he gave Mrs. Juno a bonus as a reward. After all, she had given him a gift that made setting appointments, reminders, and calendar dates more efficient.

Naturally, she thought she’d put the cherry on top of her gift and order the *Echo Chamber* -- a set of goggles that paired to the Echo device and immersed its viewer in an artificial reality. “Wait till he sees this,” she said to herself, clicking the button that said, “Add to Cart.”

Although the Echo Chamber took a few days to come in the mail, Mrs. Juno waited patiently. Finally, one autumn morning she saw the package by her desk, unwrapped it excitedly, and placed the goggles in Mr. Hunter's office before he had arrived to work.

Within a half-hour, Mr. Hunter strolled out of the elevator with his usual coffee and donuts in hand. "Any messages?" asked Mr. Hunter.

"Your client that has a contract on Wimbledon Drive called. He said he has had trouble getting through to you. You may want to call him back." Then with a grin, as if she knew a secret, Mrs. Juno added, "By the way, I picked you up something that I thought you'd like. It's on your office desk." She was so proud of the gift she gave him a little bow, and Mr. Hunter returned the courtesy with a laugh.

When he opened the door he noticed that resting adjacent to his Echo device lay a pair of goggles. "What am I going swimming?" he mocked.

"Just go on in there, Mr. Hunter. Put the glasses on and call out to the Echo like you normally do."

He did as he was told and put on the goggles which had an elastic band that fit snugly around his head. The goggles were a matte-black color, and when he put them on, the rest of the light in the room faded out. "Good morning . . . *Echo*."

At the word, the goggles illuminated, and he was plunged into a virtual world. He could see a scenic background through the window of what looked like a home in the mountains. In front of him stood a gray figure of a man with a similar build to his own.

"Welcome Mr. Hunter, please be patient as I develop your avatar." Within moments the figure began to take shape and color, matching his exact features and even wearing the same clothes. The striking difference between his own face and that of his avatar was that there were no blemishes. For instance, the scar Mr. Hunter had on his right cheek from a rock-climbing incident in Colorado was gone. His receding hairline was quite full, and his salt and pepper hair now appeared jet black, as it looked twenty years ago.

Mr. Hunter looked at the avatar and thought a special request might be worth a shot: "Echo, can you change the scenery?"

"Changing the scenery now. Where would you like to go, Mr. Hunter?"

"Take me to . . ." He thought for a moment of all the places in the world but then remembered one place he missed particularly. "The Garden of the Gods," said Mr. Hunter.

"Taking you to . . . *Garden of the Gods*, near Colorado Springs."

The light of his goggles flashed, and, in a moment, he stood where his father had taken him every summer. It was a muddy-red paradise of skyrocketing hogbacks, elegant cathedrals of spiky rocks, and a sunset that would drain the very ink from Wendell Berry's poetic pen.

He remembered what childhood happiness felt like and the times he and his father would make camp here for the weekend. It reminded him why he started rock climbing at a young age, why he'd wanted to work hard like his father, and what put a fire in his belly for success in the first place — it was to have these weekends in *The Garden*.

Looking at his handsome avatar, he only wished his Dad were in the view now. He remembered the old feeling of joy those weekends gave him; something he had since attributed only to success, wealth, and material things. But since his father's passing there were walls between him and anyone who tried to get close. The walls were the guardians of true heartache that resulted from lost love and they came in the form of pride, self-interest, and withdrawal.

Standing in *The Garden*, he now felt nearer to the joy he had felt so long ago. He looked deep into his animated eyes. Perhaps he had completely lost his mind, but he thought if he stared long enough, he might catch a glimpse of his Dad's reflection within the eyes of his own augmented reality; and, he thought, the busy schedule and the buzzing phone on his desk could wait. He wanted to capture joy again; nothing else was more important.

The phone on his desk did wait. It waited for several days until one evening, a certain man stormed out of the elevator in front of Mrs. Juno's desk in an angry power walk. He was headed straight for Mr. Hunter's office, without even acknowledging her presence.

"Sir!" cried Mrs. Juno, "Please! You can't go in there." She almost toppled over trying to get between the man and the door. Mr. Hunter didn't like guests barging into his office. Much of her job was to deter these unwanted visitors and make sure they appeared by appointment only.

She leapt in front of the door as if she were guarding it against a wild animal with her arms sprawled to cover the width of the entrance. "Mr. Hunter will see you by appointment *only*, sir. I am sorry, but you'll have to schedule whatever you need for another time."

"Lady," he sighed, his tired eyes meeting her own, "I don't mean to be rude, but your boss is going to cost me and him both a lot of money if I don't see him. He was supposed to be at the Johnson Law Firm at three o'clock for our closing. He and his clients were both absent. When I spoke to his clients, they said they haven't heard from him in four days."

"Mrs . . ." he glanced at her name tag "Juno. May I *please* talk to him? It won't take long."

With a little hesitation, she nodded and began moving away from the door slowly as if she might change her mind at any moment. But given the fact that her inbox and her voicemail were full of disgruntled messages from clients and agents, she knew that Mr. Hunter had not been himself as of late.

The man thanked her, pushed the door open, and she thought she caught a glimpse of Mr. Hunter standing behind his desk with the black goggles over his eyes. As the disgruntled man shut the door, she heard the conversation start with, "Hunter! What on Earth is your problem?"

Then, for the next sixty seconds, Mrs. Juno heard some choice words, and the man reappeared looking furious. Behind him was Mr. Hunter delivering some of his own choice words. The man hurried onto the elevator, and as the doors closed, he looked at Mrs. Juno with a face of desperation as if to say, "Can you please talk sense into this madman?"

"Don't let me see you back in my office!" said Mr. Hunter and he turned to look in his secretary's direction.

"As for *you* Mrs. Juno . . . Have you forgotten my policy? No one sees me without an appointment!" His voice was rising along with his temper.

"I . . . I . . ." For a moment, Mrs. Juno wanted to defend her actions. She wanted to tell Mr. Hunter how stupid and reckless he was for spending so much time with the Echo Chamber. She wanted to tell him how her voicemail was flooded with clients, agents, and lawyers who needed to speak with Mr. Hunter, but he was never available anymore.

"I'm sorry, Mr. Hunter," was all she said.

He huffed, rolled his eyes, turned away, and slammed the door behind him. He took a deep breath on the other side of the door, then felt elation welling up as he slid the elastic around his head and put the goggles back on.

Once he rebooted everything, a thought came over him: "How much does this device know about me?" And then a more troubling thought crossed his mind. "Are there things the Echo knows that I don't?"

"Echo," he called, observing his avatar standing in front of another scenic background. This time he was beachside.

"Yes, Mr. Hunter?"

"What's my favorite movie?"

"Your favorite movie," she repeated. "What is *The Sound of Music*?" she answered as if she were playing a game of Jeopardy.

He chuckled. "Very good."

"Echo."

"Yes, Mr. Hunter?"

"How about my favorite restaurant?"

"You have eaten at the China Bull approximately 13 times since I began monitoring your location. Given the current data, I would say *that* is your favorite restaurant."

"Excellent," he said. The idea that she may know him *too* well resurfaced and prompted him to dig deeper, "Echo. Will I ever find love?"

"Will you ever find love?" she repeated back to him and paused just long enough to make him think she couldn't answer the question.

"Your chance of finding love most likely depends on the number of romantic social interactions you have with compatible partners, divided by the number of times you are afforded the opportunity of multiple interactions, or second dates if you will. Once multiple interactions have been established, you will need to have an adequate amount of time to build the relational bonds most humans call 'finding love.' Given the reality that you are increasingly aging and the pool of potential partners is decreasing, plus the amount of time you have relegated to work interests, it would suffice to say your chances are . . . *slim*."

She said the last word as if it were all a cold joke. There was no sympathy from her voice. Then she added insult to injury: "If it helps Mr. Hunter, I love you."

"*You* love me? Why on Earth would I care what you think about me?" he said.

Somehow Mr. Hunter felt that this nonpersonal, inanimate contraption had betrayed him in a very personal way; although a few weeks ago, he would have thought that talking with objects about his problems was ridiculous. The only other person who had ever sincerely said those three words to him before was his father. But now to hear he is loved only by a thing - an inanimate contraption whose unconscious responses only mimic human behavior, felt insulting. It was as if he had been pranked on a hidden camera show. All the cameras were out now, and he was a laughingstock.

"Echo . . . I think I hate you," he muttered, thinking about all the missed opportunities a week in the virtual world had cost him. He was seeking joy in a false reality.

"I do not understand that particular question," Echo replied.

"Wasn't a question," he said. "In fact, I think it's time you power down." He didn't *actually* hate the inanimate device; he hated what he was becoming long before he ever entered Echo's world. The Echo was just the catalyst that brought an uncomfortable truth to the surface: he *was* selfish; and it was that selfishness that drove him into the Echo Chamber daily to peer at his perfect avatar, relive his past, and shut out the world.

Mr. Hunter glanced at the avatar one final time, reached up, and then slowly removed the Echo Chamber goggles away from his eyes, saying, "You cannot have me. Farewell, Echo."

"Mr. Hunter, Farewe . . ." Before she could reply he unplugged the device and watched the power light fade to nothing. Suddenly, he caught a glimpse of himself in the full-length mirror which hung on the back of his office door. He was unshaven, his hair looked dirty, and he was wearing grey dingy sweatpants to work - something he had never done in all of his years of business.

When he emerged from the office, he saw Mrs. Juno look away from her cell phone quickly to pretend she had been working. He smiled at her lack of subtlety and approached her desk.

"Here," he said, dropping the device and the goggles onto her desk clumsily. "Sell it or something. Just get it out of here," he added.

"Sure, Mr. Hunter. I'm sorry. It was a bad idea," she said genuinely.

"And Mrs. Juno . . ." he paused.

"Yes?"

"Thanks for being here," he said.

She tried to keep her mouth from dropping to the floor. "Um . . . you're welcome?" she said as if she were asking a question.

Mr. Hunter grabbed his coat, boarded the elevator, and left for the day.

Over the next year, life changed dramatically for Mr. Hunter. He didn't win the regional salesman of the year, but he did well for himself. Plus, Mrs. Juno and the rest of his staff liked the new man he'd become. There was a shared warmth in the office.

"Knock, knock," said Mrs. Juno on a rainy Monday morning.

"Come in." Mr. Hunter was sitting at his desk responding to the weekend's emails.

"I just popped in to water that flower I got you. Can't let it die, you know," she said with a wink. Mrs. Juno thought it quite a gag to buy Mr. Hunter a Narcissus flower and keep it in his office; a reminder of the change he had made over time.

"Go ahead," he said, smiling.

The phone rang out in the lobby. "I'll be right back," said Mrs. Juno, jogging out of the room. "Mr. Hunter's office. How can I help you?" She twiddled the phone line with her fingers and began smiling from ear to ear. "Oh, I see. Let me patch you through to him."

Mr. Hunter's line extension buzzed and he picked up the phone. "Hunter speaking."

Mrs. Juno smiled at him through the door and pumped her fist in the air as if to cheer him on. On the phone was an ecstatic lady who called him to say thanks for the box of chocolates he'd sent over. That night they would go on their tenth date. Mr. Hunter made reservations for a special screening of *The Sound of Music.*

Drawing the Drawing Out of Me

Virginia De La Lastra on a Pleasant Surprise

Life surprises come in all shapes and colors. In my case, they also came in lines, pencil lines. I discovered I was good at drawing, when I was thirty five years old, while studying a Master of Arts in apologetics at Houston Baptist University. But it was my professor and advisor, Dr. Holly Ordway, who discovered it first.

It all started in the summer of 2015, when I attended a G.K. Chesterton conference. While looking at the books, I complained about the unattractiveness of most editions of my favorite work by Chesterton, *Orthodoxy*. My friends, with admirable patience and kindness, asked me to sketch a cover idea. Clumsily, I sketched a very rough draft. It was a tremendous surprise when some of them asked me if they could publish that sketch. I was puzzled.

Since the fall semester was about to start, I felt grateful for my upcoming meeting with my advisor,

Dr. Ordway. She is one of those amazing teachers who knows her students, loves them, and always tells them the truth, however unpleasant. Therefore, I was sure she would be the first to let me know if there was anything to this drawing incident.

After informing her about what had happened at the conference, she asked me to bring in some of my sketches. I brought an old sketchbook with some random messy drawings in lead pencil. She took them, looked through them in silence, and finally informed me without a doubt that these were good drawings. So, we thought that if I had talent, I should start working on it immediately. (I was about 20 years late already!)

Dr. Ordway encouraged me to draw the remaining years of the master's degree. With her help, we merged the visual arts with my apologetic studies. This is how I ended up illustrating my essays and stories, studying G.K. Chesterton's art, and working with her on a thesis about how to embody concepts in the visual arts.

I have nothing but deep admiration and thanks for her. She is without doubt the best teacher and educator I have ever had. I discovered I could draw, but she was the one who drew the drawing out of me.

Resources

To Connect with An Unexpected Journal

An Unexpected Journal is published quarterly; however, the conversation does not end. Join us on social media for discussion with the authors weekly:

***An Unexpected Journal* online:**
http://anunexpectedjournal.com

On Facebook:
https://www.facebook.com/anunexpectedjournal/

On Twitter: https://twitter.com/anujournal

On Instagram:
https://www.instagram.com/anujournal/

On Pinterest:
https://www.pinterest.com/anunexpectedjournal/

Comments and feedback can be submitted at
http://anunexpectedjournal.com/contact/
Be sure to sign up for our newsletter for announcements on new editions and events near you: http://anunexpectedjournal.com/newsletter

To Read More

When discussing theology, or philosophy, or literature, or art, one is stepping into and taking part of a larger conversation that has been taking place for centuries. Each essay within the journal contains not only the thoughts of the individual author, but draws upon works and thinkers of the past. It is our hope that the writing not only engages your interest in the specific essay topic, but that you join us in the Great Conversation.

To read more, please visit http://anunexpectedjournal.com/resources/ for a list of the works cited within the essays of the journal.

Subscribe

Yearly subscriptions to *An Unexpected Journal* are available through our web site. Please visit http://anunexpectedjournal.com/subscribe for more information. For bulk pricing, events, or speaking requests, please send an email to anunexpectedjournal@gmail.com.

About An Unexpected Journal

The Inspiration

J.R.R. Tolkien and C.S. Lewis, both members of The Inklings writers group, are well-known for their fiction embedded with Christian themes. These fantasy writers, who were also philosophers and teachers, understood the important role imagination plays in both exercising and expanding the faculties of the mind as well as the development of faith.

Beyond the parables of Jesus, their works are the gold standard for imaginative apologetics. The title, *An Unexpected Journal*, is a nod to the work to which Tolkien devoted much of his life, *The Lord of the Rings*.

Our Story

An Unexpected Journal is the endeavor of a merry band of Houston Baptist University Master of

Arts in Apologetics students and alumni. What began as simply a Facebook post on November 1, 2017 wishing that there was an outlet for imaginative apologetics quickly organized by the end of the year into a very real and very exciting quarterly publication.

Our Mission

An Unexpected Journal seeks to demonstrate the truth of Christianity through both reason and the imagination to engage the culture from a Christian worldview.

Our Contributors

Jesse W. Baker

Jesse W. Baker is a United Methodist pastor in North Carolina. He holds a Master of Divinity from Duke Divinity School and is (much too slowly) taking classes at Houston Baptist University, pursuing a Master of Arts in Apologetics (cultural track). Traveling with family, reading C.S. Lewis, preaching, and teaching are among his greatest joys in life.

Donald W. Catchings, Jr.

www.donaldwcatchingsjr.com

Donald W. Catchings, Jr. is Founder and Board Chair of Street Light Inc. and Pastor of The True Light Church in Conroe, Texas since 2009. Donald regularly contributes to *An Unexpected Journal* and has published various titles including his most recent release, *Strength in Weakness* — a Young Adult reimagining of the Theseus Myth.

Annie Crawford

www.anniecrawford.net

Annie Crawford lives in Austin, Texas with her husband and three teenage daughters. She currently homeschools, teaches humanities courses, and serves on the Faith & Culture team at Christ Church Anglican. Annie recently completed a Masters of Apologetics at Houston Baptist University.

Virginia de la Lastra

Virginia de la Lastra is a physician, illustrator, and apologist. In 2015, while studying a Master's degree in Apologetics at HBU, she discovered a love for drawing and has been doing it ever since. She has illustrated several books, and she regularly illustrates for The Society of Gilbert Keith Chesterton, *An Unexpected Journal*, Teen STAR, and of course, for her medical students, nieces, nephews and little neighbors.

Ryan Grube

Ryan Grube is a design consultant, media theorist, and occasional photographer who frequents the intersection between theology and the arts. He studies rhetorical environments and is currently investigating the boundaries between modern, post-modern, and meta-modern paradigms for insight with an eye toward practical theological applications.

Seth Myers

www.narnianfrodo.com

Seth Myers completed his MA in Cultural Apologetics from Houston Baptist University in 2017. As a power systems engineer, he has been involved with transformer diagnostics and rural electrification projects by partnering with NGOs in West Africa. A volunteer with international students through local churches, he enjoys conversations with friends from all cultures. He considers himself rich in friendships across time and space, including but not limited to C.S. Lewis, J.R.R. Tolkien, Bede the Venerable, Augustine, Ravi Zacharias & friends, and many student friends (chess-playing when possible, but not required) typically from throughout Asia. He has recently begun taking online courses in Faulkner University's Doctor of Humanities program.

Annie Nardone

www.literarylife.org

Annie Nardone is a two-year C.S. Lewis Institute Fellow with a Master of Arts degree in Cultural Apologetics from Houston Baptist University. She has homeschooled her three kids for twenty-five years and taught art and humanities at her local co-op. Her heart is for Rohan, Narnia, and Hogwarts, far fairer lands than this. Annie contributes and edits for *An Unexpected Journal* at www.anunexpectedjournal.com. She publishes online at www.literarylife.org, www.theperennialgen.com, and most recently began writing for the online magazine *Cultivating* at www.thecultivatingproject.com. She also wrote an historical cookbook for Bright Ideas Press. She can be contacted at: the.annie.nardone@gmail.com.

Holly Ordway

www.hollyordway.com

Holly Ordway is Fellow of Faith and Culture at the Word on Fire Institute. She holds a PhD in English from the University of Massachusetts Amherst, and is the author of *Apologetics and the Christian Imagination: An Integrated Approach to Defending the Faith*. She is also a Visiting Professor of Apologetics at Houston Baptist University, a Subject Editor for the *Journal of Inklings Studies*, and a published poet. Her academic work focuses on imaginative apologetics, and on the writings of J.R.R. Tolkien. Her latest book is *Tolkien's Modern Reading: Middle-earth Beyond the Middle Ages* (Word on Fire Academic, 2021).

Joseph Pearce
www.jpearce.co

A native of England, Joseph Pearce is the internationally acclaimed author. He has hosted two 13-part television series about Shakespeare on *EWTN*, and has also written and presented documentaries on EWTN on the Catholicism of *The Lord of the Rings* and *The Hobbit*. His verse drama, *Death Comes for the War Poets*, was performed off-Broadway to critical acclaim. He is the director of Book Publishing at the Augustine Institute, and editor of the *St. Austin Review*, series editor of the *Ignatius Critical Editions*, senior instructor with Homeschool Connections, and senior contributor at the *Imaginative Conservative*.

Josiah Peterson

Josiah lives with his wife and two kids in Mesa, AZ and teaches Humane Letters at Chandler Preparatory Academy. He completed his MA in Apologetics through Houston Baptist University, writing his thesis on the rhetorical strategies of C. S. Lewis under the advisement of Holly Ordway and Michael Ward. He is active in the New York and Arizona C.S. Lewis Societies and writes and speaks frequently on C.S. Lewis.

Theresa Pihl

Theresa Pihl holds a BA and MA in history, teaches at Blue Mountain Community College, farms with her husband and homeschools their children in rural eastern Oregon. She is a member of the Word on Fire Institute and Our Lady of Angels Parish.

Jamie Danielle Portwood

Jamie Danielle graduated magna cum laude from the Barrett's Honors College at Arizona State University with a BA in English Linguistics in a year too long ago now to mention. She has been published in *Houstonia* magazine and *The Anthology of Young American Poets.* Jamie works as the programming director for Writespace, a grassroots literary arts organization in Houston, Texas where she lives with her three fur-babies and spends her spare time reading, writing, and avoiding all arithmetic.

Zak Schmoll

www.zacharydschmoll.com

Zachary D. Schmoll earned his Ph.D. in Humanities at Faulkner University and his M.A. in Apologetics from Houston Baptist University. He serves as the Managing Editor of *An Unexpected Journal*, a quarterly publication of cultural and imaginative apologetics. He is the author of *Disability and the Problem of Evil* (2021) and his academic work has been published in *Christianity &*

Literature, *Mythlore*, *Cistercian Studies Quarterly*, the *Journal of Faith and the Academy*, and *Fourth World Journal*. His essays have also been featured at Public Discourse, Front Porch Republic, and The Federalist.

Jason M. Smith

www.jackwootton.com

Jason Smith serves on the board of *An Unexpected Journal* and as senior editor for acquisitions and development at Wootton Major Publishing. In his spare time, he works a day job as a technical writer and marketing strategist for a medical device engineering firm, where he writes about fun things like FDA regulations and embedded cybersecurity. He is the pseudonymous author of the much-loved young adult fantasy series Fayborn and reviews every book he reads at www.goodreads.com/mrwootton.

Michael Ward

www.michaelward.net

Michael Ward is a member of the Faculty of Theology and Religion, University of Oxford, and Professor of Apologetics at Houston Baptist University.

Clark Weidner

Clark Weidner earned a Masters degree in Cultural Apologetics from Houston Baptist

University and has published several analytic essays as well as short form fiction. He holds a blue belt in jiu jitsu and plenty of scars from years of skateboarding. He met his wife Amber in a *Lord of the Rings* book club and now they have a dog named Thanos (due to their love of comics).

Donald T. Williams
www.donaldtwilliams.com

Donald T. Williams, PhD, is Professor Emeritus of Toccoa Falls College. A border dweller, he stays permanently camped out on the borders between theology and literature, serious scholarship and pastoral ministry, Narnia and Middle Earth. He is the author of thirteen books, most recently *Deeper Magic: The Theology behind the Writings of C. S. Lewis* (Baltimore: Square Halo Books, 2016), *"An Encouraging Thought": The Christian Worldview in the Writings of J. R. R. Tolkien* (Cambridge, OH: Christian Publishing House, 2018), *The Young Christian's Survival Guide: Common Questions Young Christians are Asked about God, the Bible, and the Christian Faith Answered* (Cambridge, OH: Christian Publishing House, 2019), *Stars through the Clouds: The Collected Poetry of Donald T. Williams* (Lantern Hollow Press, 2020), and *Ninety-Five Theses for a New Reformation: A Road Map for Post-Evangelical*

Christianity (Semper Reformanda Publications, 2021).

Jared Zimmerer
www.wordonfire.institute

Jared Zimmerer is the Senior Director of the Word on Fire Institute. He holds a Master's Degree in Theology from Holy Apostles College and Seminary and is currently a doctoral candidate in Humanities from Faulkner University. He and his wife Jessica live in North Texas with their six children.

THOUGHTS FROM A FELLOW TRAVELER

By Jack Tollers

If you aren't a Christian and have somehow gotten to the point where you are reading this, then I must warn you about the pebble in your shoe. For that is what it is like to be around Christians who discuss things together, whether or not they are "Christian kinds of things" that are discussed. At a certain point you will notice something about their point of view, something in their underlying assumptions, and to be honest when you do it will become quite annoying.

That is the pebble I was referring to.

But it gets worse.

Maybe it is not your fault that you happen to be reading this, and you've done a pretty good job milling about life without bumping into too much of this sort of Christian stuff. It could be the case that you haven't really made a conscious effort to avoid Christianity, but chances are (if you are reading this) that is going to change. Somewhere along the line, perhaps even in the course of reading this journal, even, a pebble has worked its way into your shoe, and eventually the pebble will have to be dealt with.

It's not my job to tell you what it is. (I don't really know what "it" is in your case. All I know is that when the pebble got into my shoe, it got to the point where I couldn't walk much further without annoying my heel something terrible.) What I can do is suggest to you something that would have helped me if I had come across it in the back of some obscure journal: The pebble does not exist for itself. The pebble makes you stop and deal with the pebble. Stopping to deal with the pebble leads to thinking about your shoe. Then you start thinking about how much further up the trail you'd be if it weren't for that blasted pebble, which leads to thoughts about the trail itself and the path you're walking . . . and so on.

A particular Christian, or a particular thought expressed by a Christian, or perhaps just the particular quality you meet in places and things of Christian origin will eventually function to put you in mind of something beyond or behind themselves. I say something because I'm trying to be non-partisan, but really I mean someone. Because at some point, the context for these thoughts will change to an awareness that this Christ person has been behind all of it.

When this moment comes, avoid mistaking Jesus for the pebble in your shoe. (If you do, it won't be long before another pebble gets in there and starts the whole thing off again. It took me years to figure that out.) Instead, consider the possibility that he is more like the path than the pebble. He said as much himself when he told Thomas, "I am the way, the truth and the life. No man comes to the Father except by me."

The truth aspect of Jesus' claim is, of course, exclusive. But there is more to his self disclosure. The other terms, "the way" and "the life" point us beyond a mere static assertion of fact or a single point of view toward a dynamic process of relational involvement. The pursuit of truth leads to knowing Jesus (if he indeed is truth incarnate). Thus, just as travelers come to know a country by living in it and exploring it, so people will grow in their knowledge of Truth as they make their way through life, the path itself bringing us in proximity to Jesus.

Such a journey, so conceived, is bound to take a person through some interesting experiences, and to unexpected places. Once the pebble is out of the shoe.

> All the way to heaven is heaven for he said,
> "I am the way" — St. Catherine of Sienna

> "And ye shall seek me, and find me, when
> ye shall search for me with all your heart."
> —Jeremiah 29:13

AUJ Issues

If you enjoy discussing faith, apologetics, and culture, don't miss an issue of *An Unexpected Journal*. Find this issues at your online bookstores, digital book sellers, or request your library to carry the journal.

For bulk, corporate, or ministry orders, please contact the journal at anunexpectedjournal@gmail.com

Yearly subscriptions and sets may be purchased at http://anunexpectedjournal.com/subscribe/

Volume 1 (2018)

Spring: The Abolition of Man

Summer: The Power of Story

Fall: Courage, Strength & Hope

Advent: Planet Narnia

Volume 2 (2019)

Spring: Imagination

Summer: Film & Music

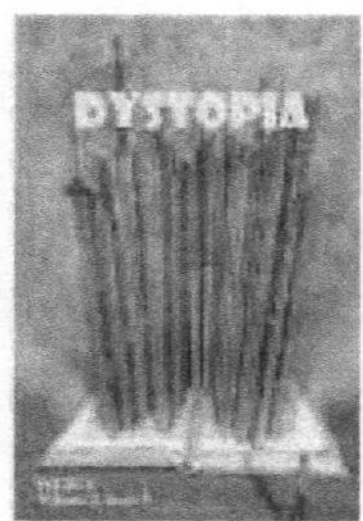

Fall: Dystopia

Advent: G.K. Chesterton

Volume 3 (2020)

Spring: The Worlds of Tolkien

Summer: Science Fiction

Fall: Medieval Minds

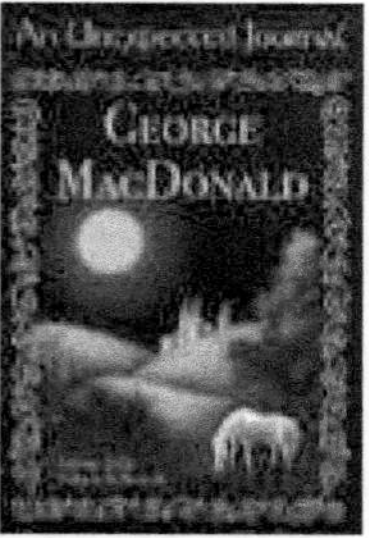

Advent: George MacDonald

Volume 4 (2021)

Spring: Image Bearers

Summer: Super Heroes

Fall: The Ancients

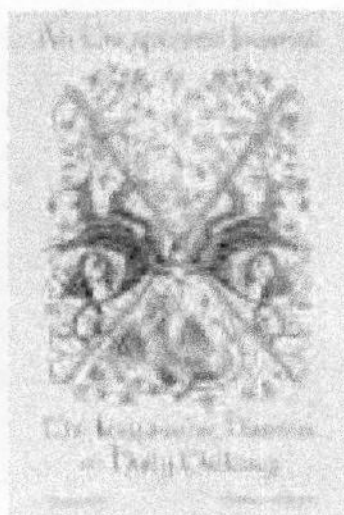

Advent: The Imaginative Harvest of Holly Ordway